CONTENTS

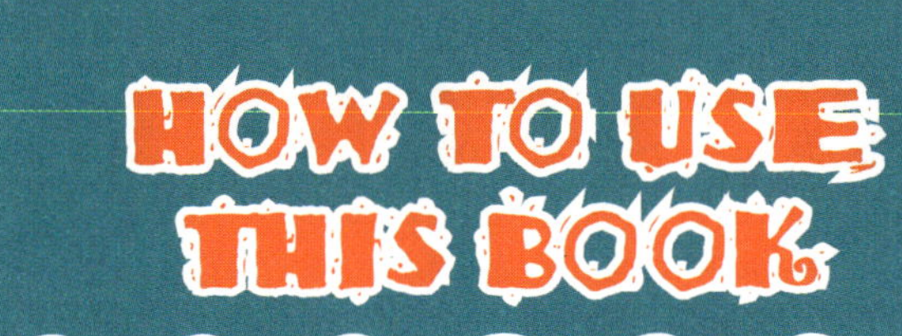

General Capabilities form one dimension of the Australian Curriculum, the others being the Learning Areas and the Cross-Curriculum Priorities. General Capabilities are taught through the content of the Learning Areas and involve knowledge, skills, behaviour and dispositions.

There are seven General Capabilities, and this *Targeting General Capabilities* Assessment book examines two of them: Critical and Creative Thinking, and Ethical Understanding. The two General Capabilities are further divided into their elements: seven in all. Each unit begins with a stimulus, followed by assessable activities that examine the element through the different Learning Areas. The table below provides a quick page reference to the different Learning Areas examined via each General Capability element in this book. You will find the relevant links to the Australian Curriculum at the beginning of each section.

Unit	Elements	English	HASS	HPE	Maths	Science	Tech	The Arts
Critical and Creative Thinking								
1	Inquiring, exploring and organising information and ideas	4	7					
2	Generating ideas, possibilities and actions	10, 12			13		14	
3	Reflecting on thinking and processes			16		20	18	18
4	Analysing, synthesising and evaluating reasoning and procedures	22, 25	22					25
Ethical Understanding								
5	Understanding ethical concepts and issues	37, 41	39					
6	Reasoning in decision-making and actions	43, 46		43	46			
7	Exploring values, rights and responsibilities	49, 51	54	49	51			

On the last page of each unit, space is allocated for self-reflection. Students have the opportunity to explore what they have learnt about each element and to record their thoughts.

There is an assessment section at the end of each General Capability where tasks are tailored to the sub-elements, rather than through the lens of a specific Learning Area. This consolidates students' understanding of the concepts and provides guidance for further reflection.

Critical & Creative Thinking

Through developing Critical and Creative Thinking Capability, children learn to generate and evaluate knowledge, clarify concepts and ideas, seek possibilities, consider alternatives and solve problems. As outlined in the curriculum, the elements and sub-elements are:

Inquiring, exploring and organising information and ideas — pose questions; identify and clarify information and ideas; organise and process information

Generating ideas, possibilities and actions — imagine possibilities and connect ideas; consider alternatives; seek solutions and put ideas into action

Reflecting on thinking and processes — think about thinking (metacognition); reflect on processes; transfer knowledge into new contexts

Analysing, synthesising and evaluating reasoning and procedures — apply logic and reasoning; draw conclusions and design a course of action; evaluate procedures and outcomes

English – Literacy

Australian Curriculum Links: *Year 3 ACELY1680 / Year 4 ACELY1692*

THE EFFECTIVE DETECTIVE

Missing Person – International – Post **BOOK OF FACES**

Missing Person – International

18 hrs

Have you seen Morgan?

Lost Australians' Police

19 hrs

Morgan Bushman's disappearance is out of character, and we are appealing for public assistance to help locate him. The 25-year-old was last seen boarding a Qantas flight to Osaka seven days ago.

Morgan's rucksack has been found, but the only clue found in the bag was a diary with notes about the places he had visited in his recent travels around the world. His family has not heard from him for more than a week, and he hasn't posted his regular diary entries to the Book of Faces. The family is very worried. Please share.

Contact Lost Australians' Police Office at 00112110.

We cannot locate a photo of Morgan at this stage; however, our police artist is drawing a likeness from descriptions given by friends and relatives.

Picture of Morgan Bushman

Description

Face shape – oval
Hair – black, curly
Nose – long and wide
Eyes – brown and wide apart
Lips – thin
Mouth – wide
Chin – pointed
Facial hair – bushy eyebrows
Clothing – last seen wearing an Akubra hat and carrying a rucksack

Lost-Australians-Police.org.au

3 likes 1 comment 2 shares

Read the description of Morgan Bushman in the Book of Faces post and draw a picture of him to help the police in their search.

English has borrowed many words from other languages. For example, kindergarten comes from the German language (kinder means children and garten means garden). Another borrowed English word is autumn, which is French. Read Morgan's diary and work out what countries Morgan has visited recently. The clues will be in the words Morgan used in the diary. As an Effective Detective, you must look at the underlined words and track down the country these words originally come from. When you find out the country of origin, write it next to the diary entry below.

HINT: Use a dictionary or web browser to look up the foreign words.

DIARY ENTRY	COUNTRY
October 11 - Dear Diary, it's finally happening. I'm ready to board the flying kangaroo! I hope I can see the Opera House as we fly northwards.	
October 12 - Dear Diary, that was a long flight. I can't wait to get my first taste of sushi and join my friends to do some singing at the karaoke bar. We might even go to a club and practise our karate. I fly out in 2 days.	
October 14 - Dear Diary, our landing was rough because a typhoon was expected. I am so hungry I could eat 10 dim sums. I would even fight the Kung Fu panda for them. Ha ha.	
October 21 - Dear Diary, I am on a diet, but I can't pass up eating at one of the hundreds of frankfurt carts here. There goes the diet. I had two frankfurts with mustard and sauce and put two more in my rucksack for later. Meeting up with my cousin who lives here and is a kindergarten teacher. Stopped at the delicatessen to get some dinner for us. Tonight she says she's going to teach me to dance a waltz.	
October 25 - Dear Diary, I was so hungry after exploring the Colosseum and throwing coins in the Trevi Fountain that I just had to find a pizzeria. My friend had said that the Pizzeria Trieste serves the best pizza and cappuccino in the land. Their spaghetti is bella! Here's a cartoon of me eating spaghetti, the local way.	
October 30 - Dear Diary, Bonjour. Guess where I am? I am really enjoying eating the local food in all the countries I am visiting. First stop is a café near the Eiffel Tower where I will rendezvous with my friend who works for the national ballet company. She has promised me the best croissant I have ever tasted.	
November 5 - Dear Diary, Hola! Guess where I am now? I really need a siesta on the patio of the hotel before I go and check out the piñata display. I wonder if they will let us break one open. I can't leave without having a bowl of paella, with chorizo sausage.	

Inquiring, exploring & organising

3 Re-read the diary entries and mark Morgan's travel route on the map below to find out in which country Morgan was last seen. Put a circle around the country in which Morgan was last seen.

HINT: Use an atlas or online map to help with this task.

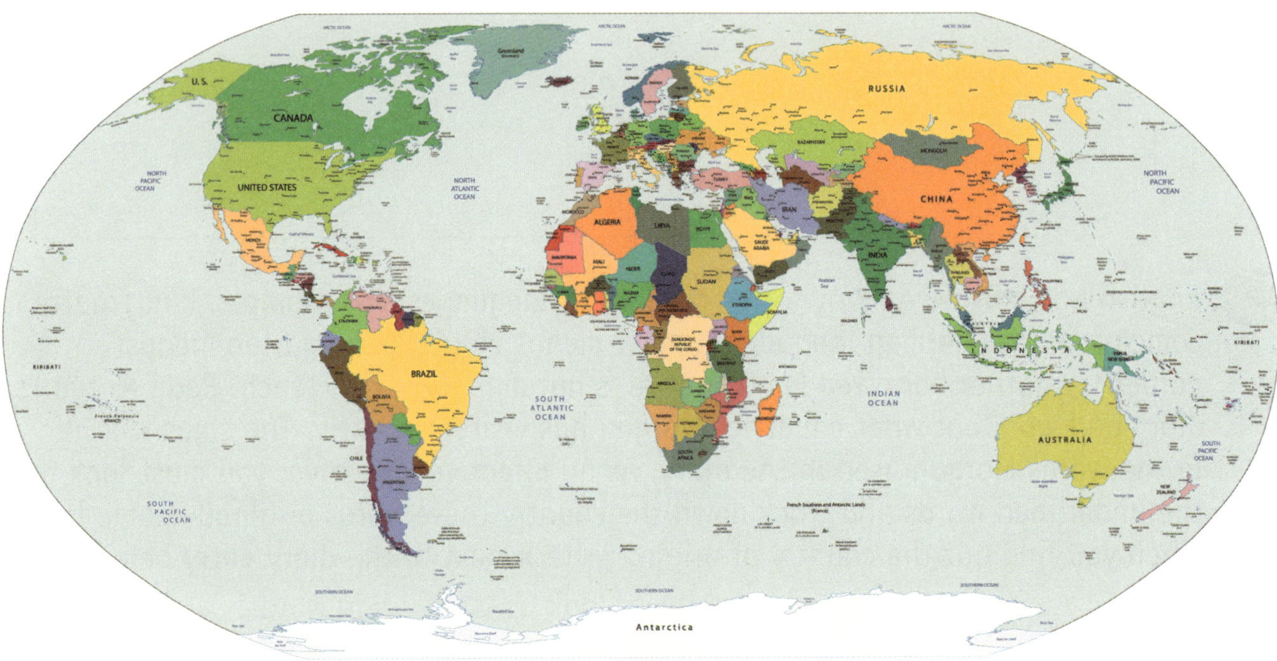

4 When the police inspected Morgan's diary closely, they found another entry Morgan had written on the last page. Read the entry below.

November 10 - Dear Diary, Today, I am heading to Gibraltar to catch the ferry to Tangiers. A whole other continent to explore. Stay tuned, diary, for my next adventure story: Morgan's African adventure!

Use the map provided to find out what country Morgan travelled to, on the ferry. The white lines show the ferry routes. Write your answer below.

____

TARGETING GENERAL CAPABILITIES: CRITICAL THINKING AND ETHICAL UNDERSTANDING YEARS 3–4 © PASCAL PRESS ISBN: 978-1925726-244

HASS – Civics and Citizenship

Australian Curriculum Links: *Year 3 ACHASSK071 / Year 4 ACHASSK092*

WHERE IN THE WORLD IS MORGAN BUSHMAN?

What is the difference between a rule and a law?

When you play a game, there are rules on how to play. When you are learning, you can find rules that help you, for example, rules for spelling. Rules are made by one person or a small group of people. However, the rules that you need to think about in this exercise are rules that are about your behaviour. A rule is how adults teach children how to behave.

At home, you may have had a rule when you were younger, for example, 'Don't run in the house!' This rule protected you from falling and getting hurt. Children are also given rules on how to treat others. You have learnt that it is wrong to hit others and that it is good to share. School children can help their teacher make the rules for the class. These rules can include raising your hand to speak and respecting others.

1 Think about the rules you have at home. Write two home rules in the space below and then write why you think those rules were made. An example has been written to show you what to do.

Rule	Reason for the rule
Children are not allowed to drive a car.	Children are too young to know how to operate and control a car. They could be hurt or cause an accident and hurt others.
1	
2	

2 What if there were no rules?
What would happen if one morning you woke up to find all the adults had left for the day and you were the only one in charge of the house? The neighbourhood children are coming to your house for a meeting about what to do, but before the meeting, you need to think about how safe the house is for children of all ages.
Below are some photos of what you found in your house. Write rules for each of the objects that will keep everyone safe. Write down what would happen if there were no rules about each object.

A 

B 

C 

D 

E 

	Rule	What would happen if there were no rules?
A		
B		
C		
D		
E		

CRITICAL & CREATIVE THINKING

Inquiring, exploring & organising

Laws are made by a government of a country or state. If someone breaks the law, then they have committed a crime and will be punished for it. There are laws about how fast adults can drive a car. If an adult is caught speeding in their car, then they could get a ticket and would have to pay money to the government as a fine. For more serious crimes, such as robbing a house or a bank, the punishment can include being sent to jail.

What happened to Morgan Bushman? Unfortunately, Morgan didn't follow the law. Read the news article below to find out what happened to Morgan and complete the tasks that follow.

TANGIERS NEWS

UNKNOWN FOREIGNER ARRESTED

November 10th

Late in the evening, an unknown tourist was arrested by customs officers at the border, with no passport or identification.

As the unidentified person left the ferry, they were asked to show their passport before they could enter the country. Unfortunately for them, they could not show the border police any paperwork.

The tourist was questioned by police and later taken to police headquarters.

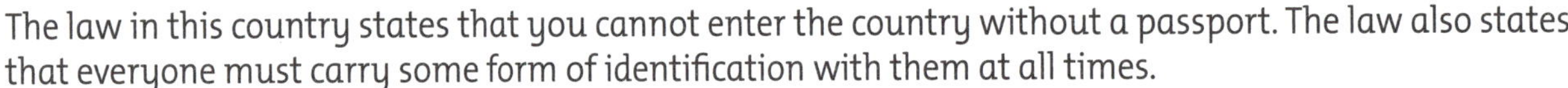

The law in this country states that you cannot enter the country without a passport. The law also states that everyone must carry some form of identification with them at all times.

As the tourist in question had nothing to prove their identity, they were charged with entering the country illegally, and taken to jail.

The unknown foreigner believes their passport and all their belongings were stolen on the ferry, pictured. The foreign tourist said their rucksack was taken while they weren't looking.

If anyone who caught the same ferry saw anything to help the police in their inquiries, please contact them immediately.

The unknown tourist will be kept in jail until authorities can prove their identity.

3 While in jail, Morgan Bushman met a man who promised to send a message to Morgan's family, explaining what had happened so that they wouldn't worry. The only paper they found was an old piece of paper from the back of a book. If you were Morgan, what would you write? Use the scrap of paper below to write your letter.

TARGETING GENERAL CAPABILITIES: CRITICAL THINKING AND ETHICAL UNDERSTANDING YEARS 3–4 © PASCAL PRESS ISBN: 978-1925726-244

WATCH OUT FOR PICKPOCKETS AND PEOPLE STEALING BAGS

Unfortunately, Morgan did not see this sign on the ferry, so the rucksack and passport were stolen. One way Morgan can get out of jail is to get a new passport because the law states that Morgan needs a passport to enter and leave the country legally.

4 You need to fill in the details in Morgan's new passport. Morgan is 21 years old today, so you will need to think about his date of birth. You know the other details. You also need to draw a picture of Morgan for the passport. Research what picture is needed in a passport. Visit this website to help you: https://www.passports.gov.au/getting-passport-how-it-works/photo-guidelines.

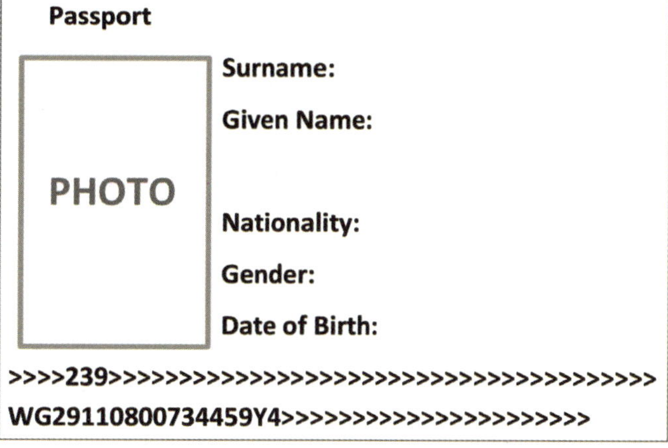
Passport

PHOTO

Surname:

Given Name:

Nationality:

Gender:

Date of Birth:

>>>>239>>>>>>>>>>>>>>>>>>>>>>>>>>>>>>>>>>>>>>

WG29110800734459Y4>>>>>>>>>>>>>>>>>>>>>>

5 Morgan is planning more travel in the future. To help Morgan and other travellers keep safe while they travel the world, write three rules in the table below that would help keep travellers safe. Write the possible consequences if Morgan does not follow the rules. One has already been done as an example.

Remember, a rule is a way of behaving that is agreed to by people taking part in an activity or belonging to a group. It is not legally binding, meaning you will not be put in jail. However, if you do not follow the rules there may be other consequences.

	Rule	Consequences for not following the rule
	Always wash your hands after being on public transport, such as ferries, planes and buses.	You may become ill and not be able to continue travelling or even end up in hospital.
1		
2		
3		

English – Literacy

Australian Curriculum Links: *Year 3 ACELY1675, ACELY1682 / Year 4 ACELY1694*

IMAGINE A DIFFERENT WAY OF THINKING – THE MESSY BEDROOM

Close your eyes and think about your bedroom. How messy or neat is it? Do you leave things on the floor? Check out the pictures of messy bedrooms above. Do these rooms look anything like yours? Compare your bedroom to the cartoon bedroom, using the table below.

My bedroom is like the cartoon bedroom because:	My bedroom is different to the cartoon bedroom because:	My bedroom is not messy like the cartoon bedroom because:
• my pets are allowed in my room. • • •	• I don't eat pizza in my room.	• I would get into big trouble if I ate food in my room.

Look closely at the cartoon drawing of a bedroom. What do you think the person who owns the room likes to do? What foods do you think they like to eat? Fill in the table below with your answers. Two answers have been done for you.

Activities/Food	Clues in the picture
pets	cat in the drawer and dog on the carpet, their bowls on the floor
pizza	box on the floor

TARGETING GENERAL CAPABILITIES: CRITICAL THINKING AND ETHICAL UNDERSTANDING YEARS 3–4 © PASCAL PRESS ISBN: 978-1925726-244

3 Many adults want children to keep their bedrooms neat and tidy, but what if being messy is actually the better way to keep your room? Look at the table below which has some points that explain why a messy bedroom is good and some points explaining why you should have a tidy bedroom. There is space to add one more idea of your own on each side.

POINTS FOR HAVING A MESSY BEDROOM	POINTS FOR HAVING A TIDY BEDROOM
Many experts believe a kid's room should be their own space to go to, so it is their decision what it looks like.	Cleaning up their room teaches children how to be responsible.
Some children want to keep their toys where they have left them because they have not finished playing with them.	A messy room could create a stressful environment.

4 After reading the points above, your job is to convince your household that a messy bedroom is better for you than a tidy one. In the space provided below, write a speech to your household to persuade them that a messy bedroom is best. Use the points in the table and any other points you can think of in your speech. Read your speech to the adults in the house to see if your argument works!

You can even film yourself in your bedroom giving your speech and play it to your household. How convincing can you be?

The Speech

Why a messy bedroom is the way to go.

____

____

____

____

____

____

Have you convinced your household? Yes / No

5 Write a reply to your speech as if you were the adult at home. You could agree with your reasoning about having a messy bedroom, or you could look at the points in the table and argue that a tidy bedroom is best. Which way will you go? Write your reply below.

If I was an adult, I would think

____

____

____

TARGETING GENERAL CAPABILITIES: CRITICAL THINKING AND ETHICAL UNDERSTANDING YEARS 3–4 © PASCAL PRESS ISBN: 978-1925726-244

Generating ideas

English – Language

Australian Curriculum Links: *Year 3 ACELA1483 / Year 4 ACELA1496*

Imagine a different way of thinking – What can't you see?

When you see a picture like the one shown here, have you ever wondered what you are not seeing? What did the original picture look like before the image was cut out? Where was this character? Well, now you have the chance. Check out the second picture below. Can you find the original character in the larger picture? Did you think it was in a claw machine for toys? Next time you see a picture, think about what it is you are not seeing. What has been cut away?

Now it's your turn. You have two pictures of a lion cub. You have to think and ask the questions, where was this lion cub and what is it that we do not see?

Think of two different places where the lion cub might be sitting.

For example, in one picture, the lion cub may be in the jungle with its family, or in a zoo or tourist park, or even in a movie scene. Be creative and draw two different pictures that show what might be missing from the picture.

Picture 1	Picture 2

What does this picture of eggs make you think? What are those eggs looking at or what have they seen?

As a writer, you have the power to make us think about the picture in any way you want. In the box below, write two more reasons for the look on the eggs' faces. Two examples have been given to jump-start your thinking.

The Eggs' Faces

They are watching a horror movie on NETFLIX!

They saw an advertisement about eating more eggs!

____

____

____

Mathematics – Measurement and Geometry

Australian Curriculum Links: *Year 3 ACMMG066 / Year 4 ACMMG091*

Imagine a different way of thinking – Symmetry

 All of the drawings below need you to use symmetry to complete them. However, before you can finish these drawings, you need to know what symmetry means. Use a dictionary or research online to find out what symmetry means. Write your answer below.

Symmetry is

____

____

 Now that you know what symmetry is, your task is to finish each of the drawings below so that the other half of the picture is symmetrical. Use the grids as a guide to help your drawing be as accurate as possible.

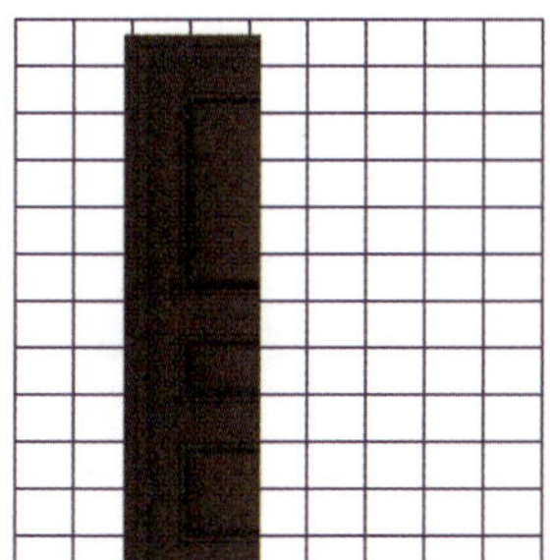  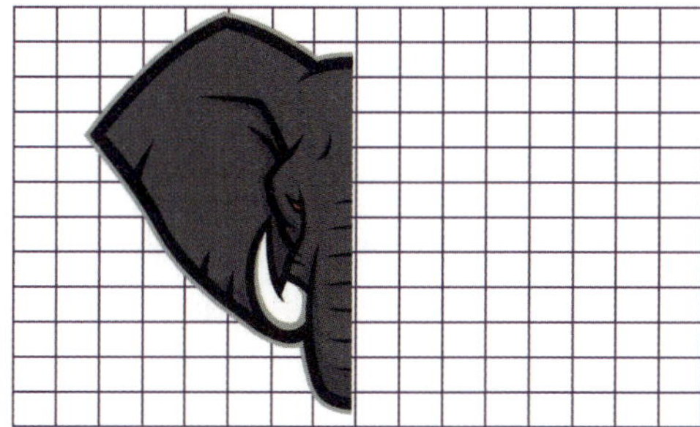

 Now it is your turn to draw a completely symmetrical picture in the grid below. Remember, to be symmetrical, each side needs to be exactly the same.

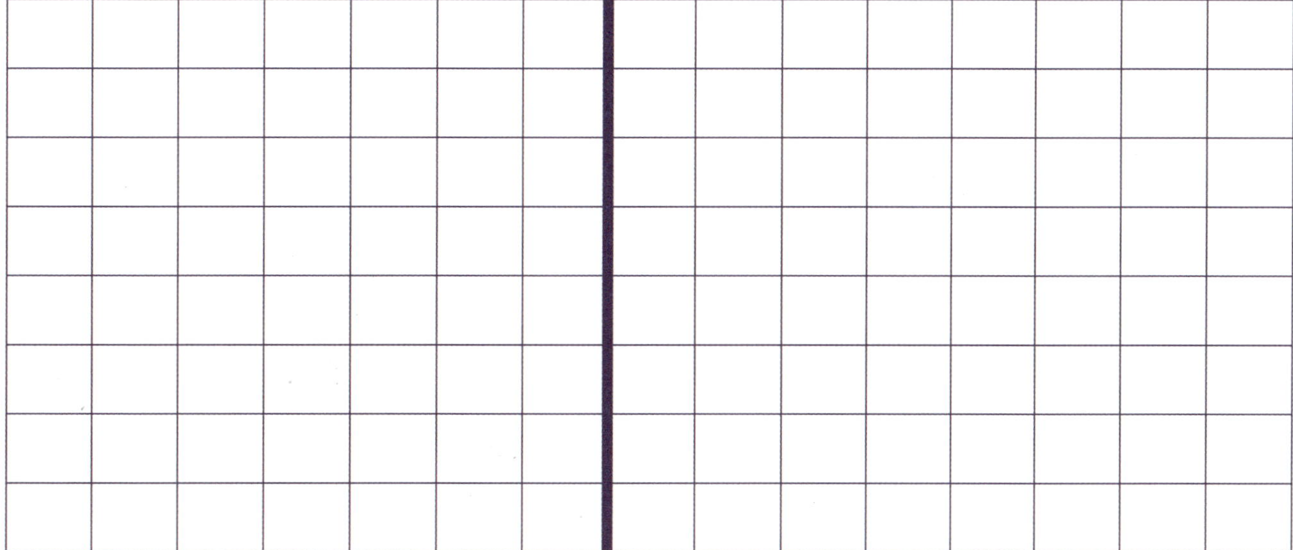

CRITICAL & CREATIVE THINKING

Technologies – Design and Technologies

Australian Curriculum Links: *Years 3 & 4 ACTDEP015*

Imagine a different way of thinking – Generating ideas

Being able to think of good ideas takes practice. It is not always easy to be creative and think of new ideas. One way to help you practise thinking creatively is to brainstorm or think about all the different ways you could use one object. For example, what are the possible uses of a paperclip? It could be used as a bookmark or to pop balloons.

Brainstorm at least four things the objects listed below could be used for. Be as creative as you can by thinking of very different ways to use the object.

a brick	a fork	a toothbrush

Imagine a different way of thinking – Combining ideas

Inventors often put two ideas together to make something new. Take the idea of a radio alarm clock. It is really an alarm clock added to a radio and there you have it: a radio alarm clock! Check out the pictures below to show how the two ideas joined together.

The Japanese have invented a word for inventions that solve a problem, but the solutions are impractical and rather useless. These inventions have to combine very different objects in an interesting way to create a new product. They call it Chindogu. Check out the website if you would like to see examples of Chindogu: https://www.languageconnections.com/blog/ten-japanese-chindogu-inventions/.

Try your creativeness by creating your own Chindogu inventions. Below are objects that you need to combine to create two new products. These objects have actually already been combined to form a Chindogu product. How would you combine them and what problem would it solve? Draw your new inventions and explain how they work. The last box is for you to think of your own Chindogu invention.

The objects are: 1 – two small funnels 2 – eye drops 3 – glasses	The objects are: 1 – two small umbrellas 2 – new shoes	The objects are: 1 ______________ 2 ______________
The problem is ...	The problem is ...	The problem is ...
The drawing of your invention.	The drawing of your invention.	The drawing of your invention.

Generating ideas

4 This time, you will start with a problem that you need to solve. The problem for you to solve is: space junk.

Every week you need to take out the rubbish from your house and put out the bins. Every week, large trucks take your rubbish away so you can have a clean and healthy house. But just imagine you lived in a part of the world where no-one ever collected your rubbish. Where would you put all the things you do not want or need anymore? Your house would become crowded and unhealthy. Now think about what happens in space if no-one collects all the manmade rubbish that is not needed anymore.

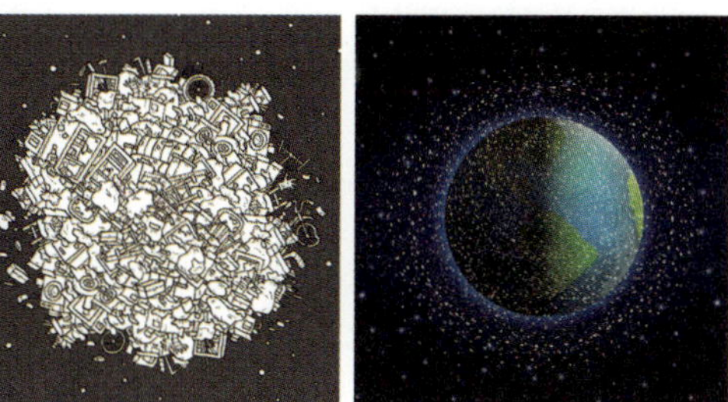

Space junk around our planet Earth is made up of old satellites that don't work anymore and parts of spaceships that are not needed. Space junk becomes dangerous for working satellites and the Space Station. This is because space junk can collide or crash into working satellites and cause a lot of problems for communication or for the astronauts on the Space Station.

To find out more, check out this BTN program on space junk: https://www.abc.net.au/btn/classroom/space-junk-clean-up/10834252. The BTN program shows a robot satellite that collected space junk. The robot used two ideas: a net and a harpoon. A harpoon is like a very large arrow. Many countries are designing ways to collect the space junk, can you help them?

5 Your task is to combine two ideas to invent a machine that will collect space junk. Write your two ideas here.

________________________ ________________________

In the space below, draw a diagram of your invention that shows how you have joined the ideas together to capture space junk.

6 Name your product ______________________________

7 You have now been asked to write a 'jingle' or song to advertise your new invention. Use one of the following ideas:

- Use the tune of Twinkle, Twinkle Little Star and change the words.
- Make a rap.
- Use any tune you wish and change the words.

Health and Physical Education – Personal, Social and Community Health

Australian Curriculum Links: *Years 3 & 4 ACPPS033, ACPPS034, ACPPS035, ACPPS036, ACPPS038*

Brave Thinking – The Masked Singers

You might have watched a show that has become very popular in many places around the world is *The Masked Singer*. This is a program where celebrities, or people who are well known by the public, dress up in very fancy costumes and sing in a competition. Many of the celebrities are not singers and they had to find the confidence to perform in front of an audience and sing. For many, the costumes helped them overcome their fears to perform because the audience did not know who they were and could judge them only on their singing ability. These people had to practise brave thinking. Someone who did just that was Sophie Monk.

Sophie Monk was one of the celebrities on *The Masked Singer Australia*. She had to show brave thinking to perform, and the dragonfly costume she wore helped her develop the confidence she needed. Sophie said, 'There's something about the disguise that makes it so much easier to just bring out confidence. You're not worrying about what people think about you. No-one was judging me. I could just sing.'

1. If you had to choose a costume to perform in, what animal would you choose to represent you and why? Think of two animals you would choose and fill in the table below.

Choice of animal	Reason why

Read the cartoon below.

1

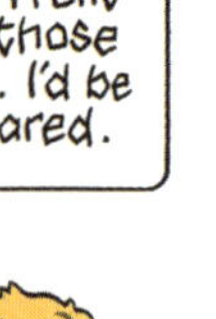

2

3

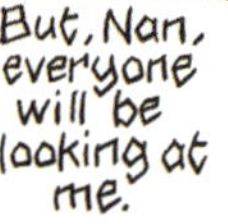

4

Source: www.ethicsfun.com

TARGETING GENERAL CAPABILITIES: CRITICAL THINKING AND ETHICAL UNDERSTANDING YEARS 3–4 © PASCAL PRESS ISBN: 978-1925726-244

Reflecting on thinking & processes

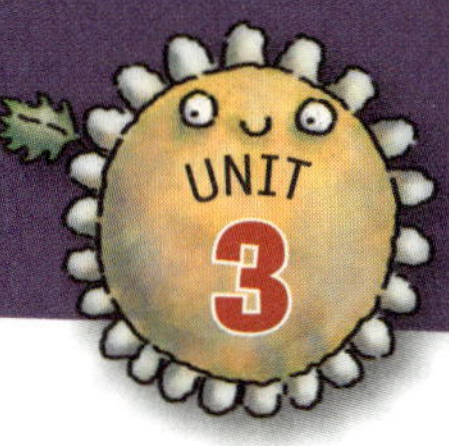

After reading the cartoon, answer the questions below.

In the first frame, **where** in the house are Mum and Larena talking? How do you know? What are the clues?

____

How does Mum know about the school choir auditions?

a) The school phoned to tell her.

b) Nan told her.

c) She read it in the school news.

d) Larena told her.

What do you think is happening in frame 2 of the cartoon?

a) Larena is imagining herself croaking like a frog at the auditions.

b) Mum is telling Larena to have more confidence.

c) Larena is explaining that she is too scared to sing in front of strangers.

d) All of the above.

By the end of the cartoon, Larena did some brave thinking, believing in herself and overcoming her fear so she could sing in the choir audition. Think of a time when you have been scared to do something, like Larena was. Fill in the table below to explain how you used your brave thinking to overcome your fear. Look at the example to guide your answer.

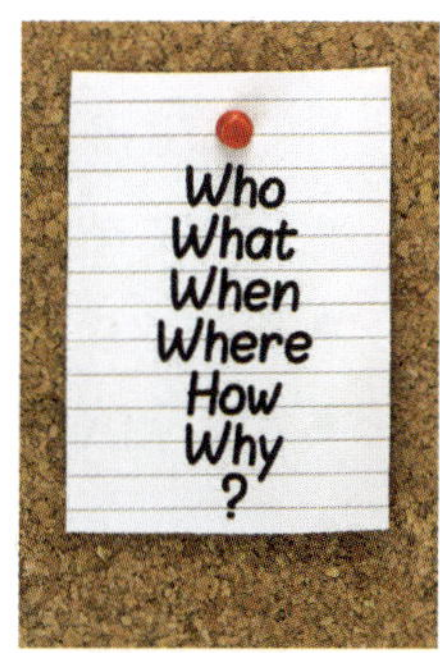

5 Ws + H

Who	What	When	Why	Where	HOW – Our brave thinking strategy
My friends and me	To dance with the class	Grade 4, last assembly of term	We were scared that people would laugh at us.	At the school assembly	We practised many times so we would be good.

Your turn

Who	What	When	Why	Where	HOW – Our brave thinking strategy

In frame 3, Larena talks to Nan and says everyone will be looking at her. Then, in frame 4, she is singing at the auditions. How do you think Nan helped Larena to find the courage to sing? Circle as many answers as you think might have happened.

a) Nan told Larena to be brave and that she belonged in the choir.

b) Nan promised Larena some money if she went to the auditon for the choir.

c) Nan helped her practise.

d) Nan told her that she was being silly.

The Arts – Visual Arts & Technologies – Design and Technologies

Australian Curriculum Links: *Years 3 & 4 ACAVAM111, ACTDEP015*

Brave Thinking – Poster

1. Brainstorm at least three ideas of what advice you could give to other students your age, on how to do brave thinking. For example, trying something they feel is difficult or seeking advice from adults about things they have to do that is hard.

i ____________________

ii ____________________

iii ____________________

2. You need to communicate these ideas through a poster. You can create a digital poster or create a poster on paper. To create an effective poster, you need to follow the criteria below:

- Draw a picture that will get people interested. Use bright colours!
- Write a headline for the poster—nice and big so it gets attention.
- Put in your message what you want people to do or remember about your topic.
- Be creative.
- Be clear. Can your message be read and understood by everyone?
- Use headings and sub-headings.
- If you are not creating a digital poster, create a rough draft before you do the final poster.

3. To help you think about what makes a good poster, you are going to judge the posters on the next page. These posters have been designed by students. Think about what makes a good poster and rank them. Put them in order of most effective (number 1) to the least effective (number 6). Use the table below to record your answers. In the last column, write some reasons for the way you ranked them.

Poster	Rank 1-6	Reasons for decision
A		
B		
C		
D		
E		
F		

TARGETING GENERAL CAPABILITIES: CRITICAL THINKING AND ETHICAL UNDERSTANDING YEARS 3–4 © PASCAL PRESS ISBN: 978-1925726-244

A

B

C

D

E

F

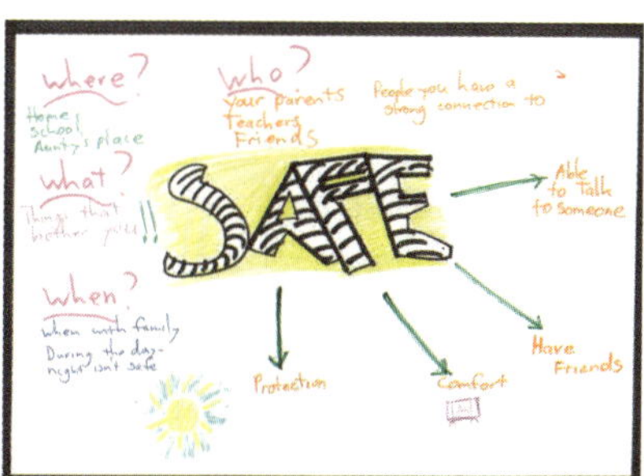

Your Poster

Science – Chemical Understanding and Inquiry Skills

Australian Curriculum Links: *Year 3 ACSSU046, ACSIS053, ACSIS215 / Year 4 ACSSU074, ACSIS064, ACSIS216*

Brave Thinking – Scientists and Inventors

If you want to be a scientist or an inventor, you need brave thinking. You need brave thinking because you can make mistakes as things do not always turn out the way you expect. Check out Kid President's video to find some interesting information about being an inventor: https://www.youtube.com/watch?v=75okexRzWMk. If scientists and inventors make mistakes and discoveries, and learn from them, then what happens to the mistakes and discoveries?

Look at the list of items below.

slinkies	potato chips	play dough	microwave oven
post-it notes	cornflakes	penicillin	non-stick pans
matchsticks	safety glass	popsicles – ice blocks	silly putty

What do all these things have in common?

____

Did you work out what they all had in common? That's right, they were all invented or discovered by accident! Scientists and inventors were looking to create something but ended up with something else. It took brave thinking to be able to use their mistakes. The links below will give more information about these 'accidental inventions'. View the videos with an adult:

https://www.mentalfloss.com/article/85286/8-things-invented-accident

https://www.cbc.ca/kidscbc2/the-feed/oops-5-cool-things-invented-completely-by-accident

Now it's time for you to do your own research. Find out how Velcro was discovered. Research and write down the information below.

What I found out about how Velcro was discovered:

____

____

Brave Thinking and the Oobleck

For years, people had known that corn flour mixed with water creates a mixture that does not act like a normal liquid or solid. The name of this mixture is oobleck. You might wonder how it got this strange name. Not only did Dr. Seuss write *The Cat in the Hat*, but he also wrote a book, *Bartholomew and the Oobleck*, where a gooey green substance, which he called oobleck, falls from the sky and causes lots of problems in the story.

Scientists had been investigating oobleck and found that, under certain conditions, they were able to poke holes in the fluid that would stay there! You certainly can't do this with water.

Check out the videos below that will provide you with more information about oobleck:

https://www.canr.msu.edu/news/science_ideas_for_young_children_part_9_oobleck

https://www.thebestideasforkids.com/how-to-make-oobleck/

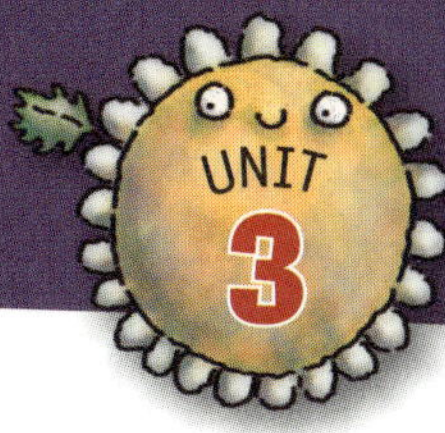

Your oobleck investigation

Now it is your turn to mix up some oobleck. Before you make the mixture, you need to fill in Step 1 of the Predict, Explain, Make, Observe and Explain (again). Now you are doing a PEMOE, like a real scientist.

PEMOE TABLE

My oobleck investigation
Step 1 Predict Write or draw all the things you think you will see when you start making the mixture.
Step 2 Explain Write the reasons you think it will happen this way.
Step 3 Make the mixture Oobleck recipe: • Pour 2 cups of corn flour into a large bowl. • Add 1 cup of water. You can add a few drops of food colouring to the water if you like. • Stir to combine the water and corn flour.
Observe Draw or describe what you see when you play with oobleck. For example, what happens when you poke it, push it, prod it, grab a handful or let it run over your fingers?
Explain Add to or change your ideas about why it happened. You can look back at the videos to help you.

Source: adapted from POE, developed by White and Gunstone (1992)

English – Language & Literacy

Australian Curriculum Links: *Year 3 ACELA1477, ACELY1675 / Year 4 ACELA1489, ACELY1686*

HASS – Inquiry and Skills

Australian Curriculum Links: *Year 3 ACHASSI059, ACHASSI060 / Year 4 ACHASSI080, ACHASSI081*

Thinking and acting like a HERO – a High Energy Reasoning Operator

You have probably heard about heroes and have watched movies or TV shows about them. You may even know someone who is a hero in your life! Heroes may be adults in your life like your grandparents, parents or neighbours. Children and young people can also be heroes like your older brothers and sisters, friends or classmates. Sometimes your teachers or sports coaches will demonstrate the qualities of a HERO.

1 Recipe for a HERO

Because of your ability to think creatively and critically and use your reasoning, you have been selected to make a HERO using the newly invented HERO-making machine called, *THE HEROMAKA* (pronounced her – rom – ak – a).

First Step:

Choose the ingredients/qualities that you want your HERO to have and that you think are the most important. Select from the 'QUALITIES OF A HERO' list below and place them into *THE HEROMAKA*. Place one HERO ingredient into each of the cogs in the machine.

QUALITIES OF A HERO	HEROIC ACTIONS
wise	• make the world a better place
strong	• find ways to be helpful
clever	• be a leader
fearless	• care for other people's feelings and wellbeing
brave	• be a role model for everyone
reliable	• save lives
mighty	• stop disasters
daring	• be a hard worker
courageous	• help the community
inspiring	• help people learn
positive	• listen to people
friendly	• be there when people need them
organised	• be a problem solver and help others to solve problems
cooperative	• put effort into everything they do
responsible	• demonstrate common sense
patient	• always do their best
flexible	• always show respect
curious	• organise and understand information (synthesise)
creative	• work out how to solve a problem (reasoning and problem solving)
generous	• think through situations before acting (analysing)
proud	• understand when something is not working and work out new actions (evaluating procedures)
honest	
resourceful	
thinkers	

TARGETING GENERAL CAPABILITIES: CRITICAL THINKING AND ETHICAL UNDERSTANDING YEARS 3–4 © PASCAL PRESS ISBN: 978-1925726-244

THE HEROMAKA

YOUR HERO

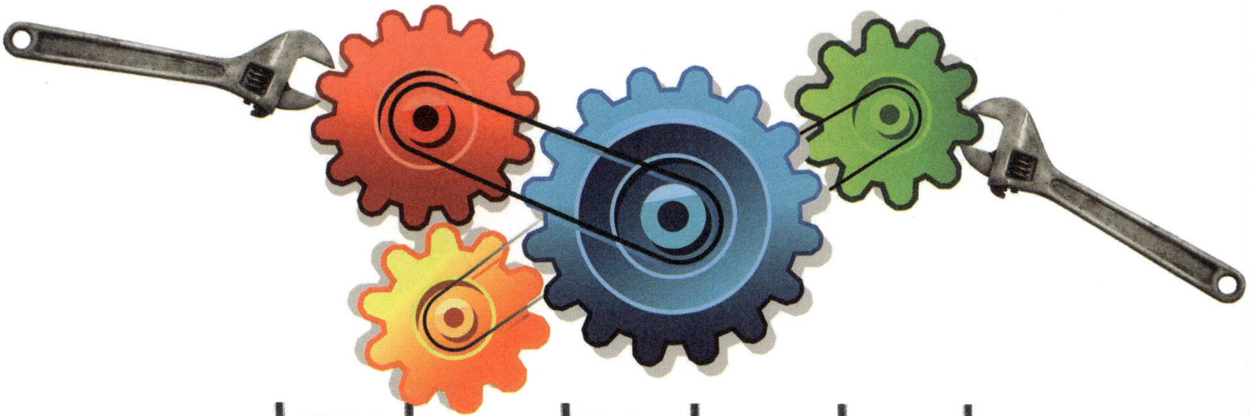

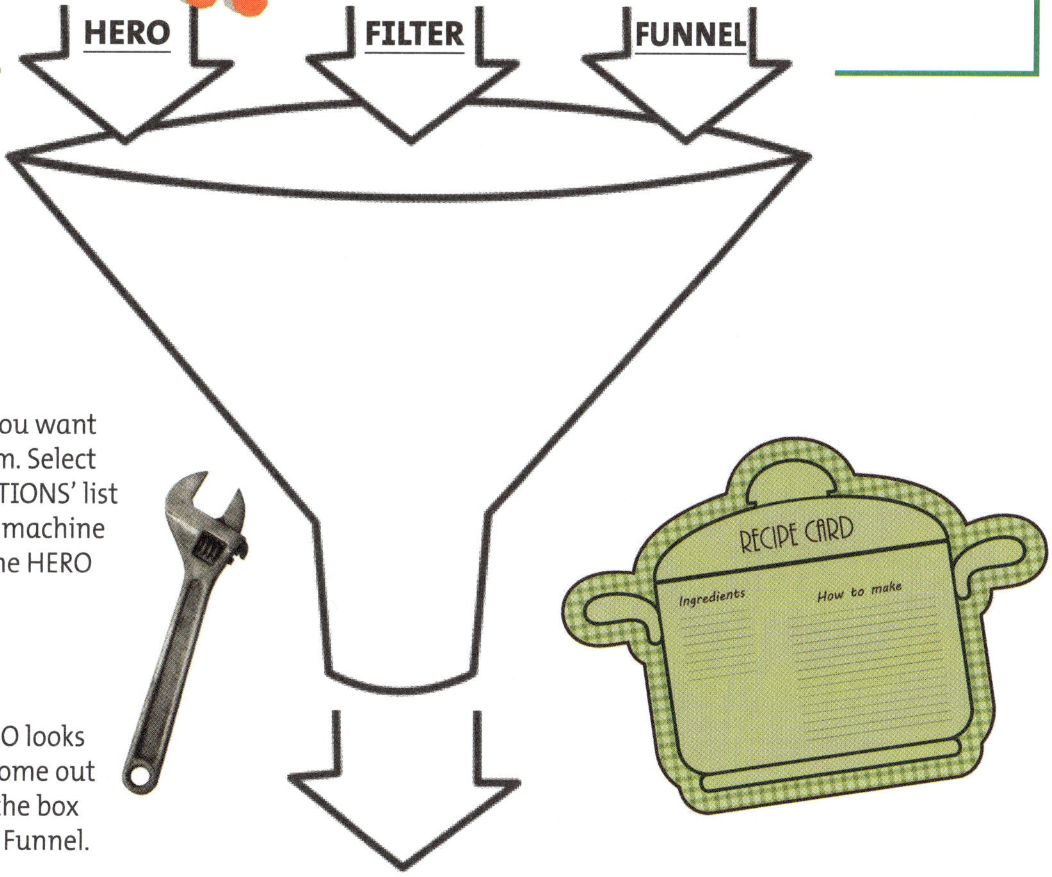

HERO **FILTER** **FUNNEL**

RECIPE CARD

Ingredients

How to make

Second Step:

Choose the actions you want your HERO to perform. Select from the 'HEROIC ACTIONS' list and add them to the machine by writing them in the HERO filter funnel.

Third Step:

Draw what your HERO looks like after they have come out of the machine. Use the box under the Hero Filter Funnel.

Analysing, synthesising & evaluating

2. For a hero to operate, they need to have a licence. The licence will allow your HERO to perform their heroic actions. To get your hero a licence, you have to go to the HERO Registration Board and fill in some forms before they will allow your hero to become a registered member. The HERO Registration Board has sent you the following information. You need to fill in the information they ask of you.

HERO REGISTRATION BOARD

Thank you for wanting to register your HERO. You need to fill in the following information:

I. Every HERO needs a heroic name. What is the name of your HERO?

____

II. You gave your HERO some heroic qualities and actions. Think of a situation or time that your HERO could use them to help others. Use the table below.

What is the problem?	What did your HERO do to help?	What heroic qualities or actions did they use?

III. There are people in your life who are heroes to you. Who in your life does your HERO remind you of? In what ways have they helped to make your life better?

Who in your life is like your HERO?	How has your HERO made your life better?

IV. How are you and the HERO you created in the HEROMAKA alike and how are you different? Use the Venn Diagram below to fill in your similarities and differences. Refer to the list of Hero Qualities and Actions on the previous page.

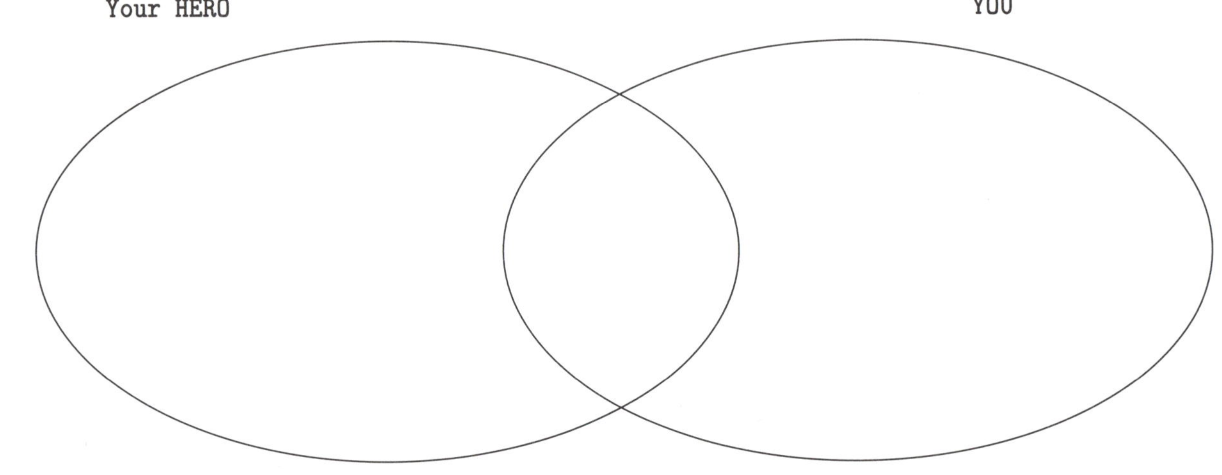

TARGETING GENERAL CAPABILITIES: CRITICAL THINKING AND ETHICAL UNDERSTANDING YEARS 3–4 © PASCAL PRESS ISBN: 978-1925726-244

The Arts – Visual Arts

Australian Curriculum Links: *Years 3 & 4 ACAVAM111, ACAVAM112*

English – Language & Literacy

Australian Curriculum Links: *Year 3 ACELA1483, ACELY1675 / Year 4 ACELA1496, ACELY1686*

Looking is not always seeing

1. Looking is not always seeing! When we look at something or even read something, we might not be aware that we are not seeing the whole picture.

   Look carefully at the image. Use your art-investigating training to write down five things you can see in the picture.

   1. ______________________________

   2. ______________________________

   3. ______________________________

   4. ______________________________

   5. ______________________________

2. What do you think this is a picture of? ______________________________

3. It may surprise you to know that you are only seeing part of the picture. To see what the whole picture is, go to the answer page for this unit. The whole picture is a picture of ____________________.

4. Before you can make decisions about what you see, hear or read, you need to make sure you get the 'whole picture'.

An example of this is the story of *The Six Blind Men* who went to visit an animal they had heard of. Each man went up to the animal and felt the animal with their hands and decided what they thought the animal was like. Each man only felt part of the animal. They could only really understand the animal if they put all their descriptions together.

Use the table below to draw what each man thought the animal was like.

Blind man	Their description of the animal	Your drawing of their descriptions
1	The animal is nothing more than a piece of old rope.	
2	The animal is like a giant snake.	
3	The animal is smooth and solid like a wall.	
4	The animal is like a huge handheld fan or like a magic carpet.	
5	The animal's leg is thick like a tree trunk.	
6	The animal is as sharp and deadly as a spear.	

Analysing, synthesising & evaluating

5 Before you make decisions about what you see, hear or read, you need to make sure you have all the information.

Now that you have heard from the six blind men, put all their information together. Can you work out the animal?

i What do you think the animal is? ______________________________

ii What makes you think that is the answer? ______________________________

6 It is now your turn to describe an animal. Just like the six blind men, you will provide pieces of information that together make up your animal. Think of an animal you want to describe. Think of four parts of the animal and what you could compare them to. Look at the table below which gives an example.

Clue 1	Clue 2	Clue 3	Clue 4	Answer
The animal is like the inside of a large feather quilt or a giant feather duster.	The animal is pointed like a sharp spear.	The animal is long, thin, scaly and powerful, like a strong stick.	The animal is like a thick snake with feathers at one end.	What am I? I am an Australian animal.

What do you think the animal in the example is? ______________________

To find out what it is and what the various parts are, you need to check the unit answer page.

7 Your turn to fill in the table. Once you have completed the table, read out your descriptions to friends and family. Can they guess your animal?

Clue 1	Clue 2	Clue 3	Clue 4	Answer

8 This may surprise you, but not everyone sees things the way you do. This is called point of view or perspective. In the story of *The Six Blind Men*, each man had their own view or perspective of the animal they went to meet. Before you can make reasonable decisions, you need to see other people's points of view or perspectives of any situation.

Looking at things from different perspectives requires reasoning, creative thinking and decision-making. Perspective means to 'look through' or 'perceive', so all the meanings of perspective have something to do with looking. Whether you are looking at an image from different viewpoints or perspectives, or you are looking at a problem situation, or listening to a person give their opinion about something, you are using perspective. To be able to draw a conclusion or make a decision, you need to gather as much information as possible.

How good are you at seeing things from a different perspective? Use the table below to draw the bed and the person in it from different positions or perspectives. The different positions are listed in the table.

Side view	Top view from the ceiling	Standing at the bottom of the bed	Lying under the bed

The story, *Fish is Fish*, by Leo Lionni is told from the very different perspectives of a fish and of a tadpole that turns into a frog. In the story, the fish is told by his friend the frog about the wonderful world out of the pond.

The book shows how the fish pictured creatures like cows, humans and birds all with fish bodies because from his point of view or perspective, his world is made up of fish-like creatures. The fish imagined that all other creatures looked like itself.

Imagine you are an emu who has never seen the ocean or any creature who lives or plays in the ocean. What if your emu self was told about sharks and surfers? Draw a shark and a surfer from the point of view of an emu, using emu-like bodies.

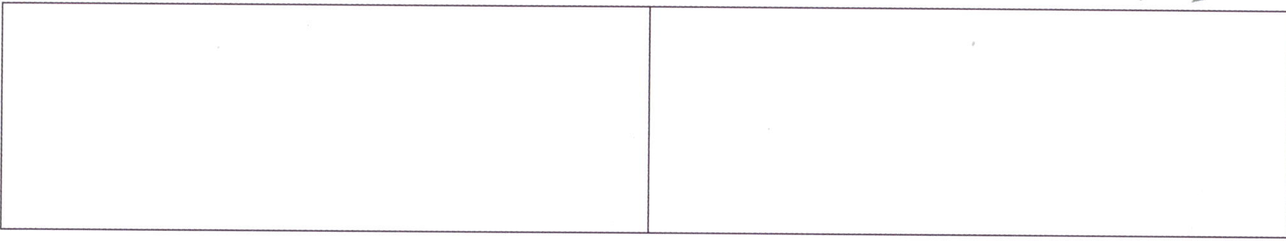

What if you could put yourself in someone else's shoes? That means thinking like them and seeing the world from their point of view.

It is your turn to imagine you are a family pet of your choice. The pet may belong to family or friends. Write a diary account of one day in the life of this pet. You may need to research your pet animal and find out about its daily activities and habits, what it likes to do, what it eats and how it lives with humans.

Inquiring, exploring & organising information & ideas – Unit 1

Pose questions / Identify and clarify information and ideas

THE EFFECTIVE DETECTIVE

This unit was about finding Morgan Bushman and being an effective detective. To do this, you had to explore and find information and then use that information in a clever way to find in which country Morgan was last seen.

1. Re-read Morgan's diary and the newspaper report on pages 5 and 8. Choose your own adventure by writing your story of what you think happened to Morgan. Choose one or more of the ideas below and write the ending of Morgan's adventure.

   a) Morgan escaped from the jail in Tangier.

   b) Morgan was issued with a new Australian passport.

   c) Morgan's rucksack was never stolen.

Organise and process information

2. Read the following information about the difference between rules and laws.

   A rule is a way of behaving that is agreed to by people taking part in an activity or belonging to a group, such as a game, sport or contest at school. It is not legally binding but may have other consequences like not being allowed to play a game, join a club or do an activity.

   Laws are made by government and are legally binding. If you break a law, you can be fined or even jailed.

TARGETING GENERAL CAPABILITIES: CRITICAL THINKING AND ETHICAL UNDERSTANDING YEARS 3–4 © PASCAL PRESS ISBN: 978-1925726-244

Look at the rules and laws in the pictures below and then sort them using the diagram provided.

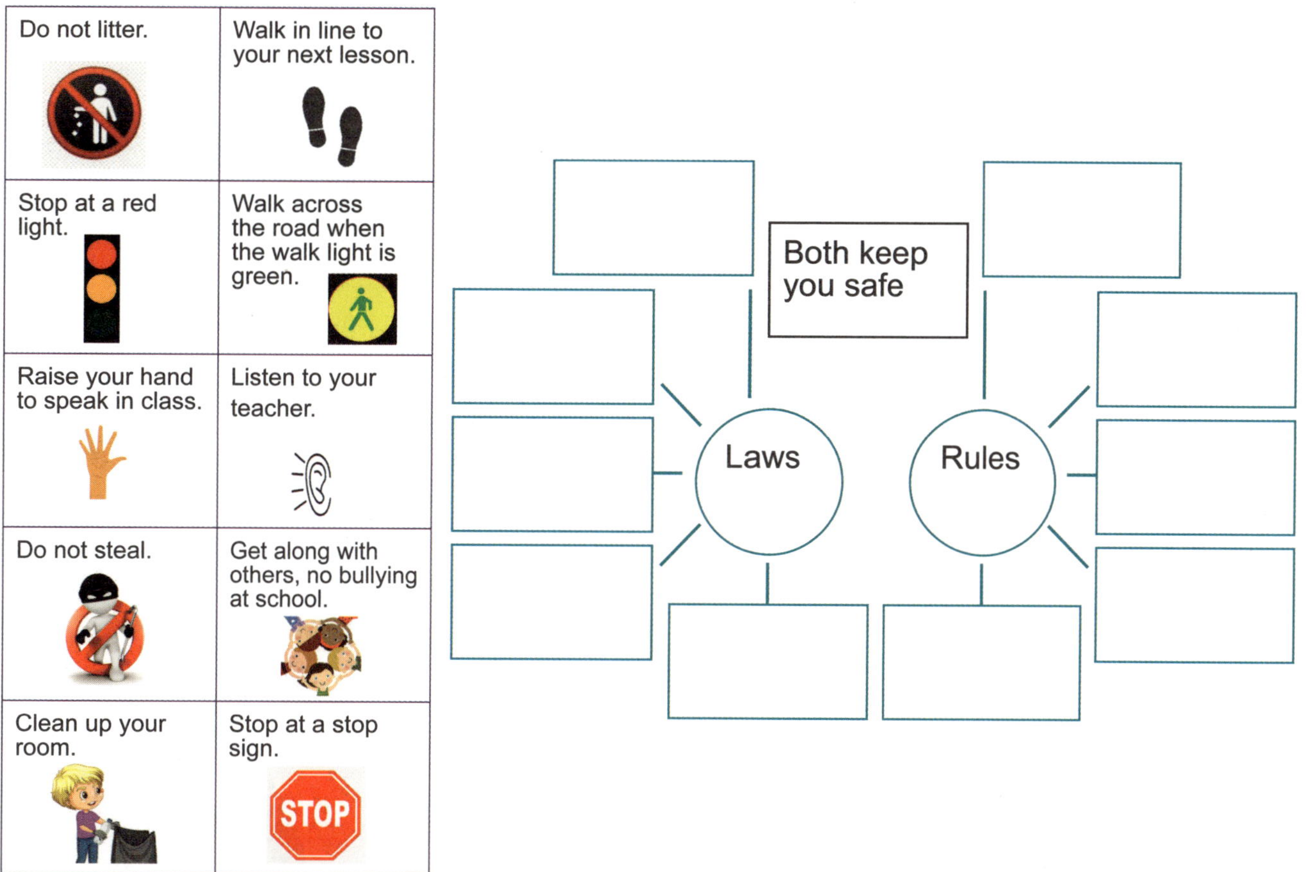

It is time to check what you have learnt about rules and laws. How many of the quiz questions can you answer? Check your answers when you have finished.

Quiz Questions – Is it a rule or a law?

	Question	Rule/Law	Who enforces it?	Consequences of breaking the rule/law
1	Drive at a reduced speed in school zones.			
2	Raise your hand to speak in class.			
3	You must go to bed by 8:30 pm.			
4	You must not steal from others.			
5	Tackling is not permitted.			
6	No littering on beaches.			

Generating ideas, possibilities & actions – Unit 2

Imagine a different way of thinking

In this unit, you had to imagine a different way of thinking. You looked at other possibilities and thought about new ideas and different ways of doing things. For example, thinking about why having a messy bedroom could sometimes be okay and convincing someone else of that idea. We also looked at pictures in a different way. For example, when looking at pictures you have to think about what might not be included in the picture and why. We also looked at symmetry and recognised that some images can be made so that each side is a mirror image of the other.

Imagine possibilities and connect ideas

Investigate to answer this question: Is your face symmetrical? Refer back to page 13 to remind yourself about symmetry. For this activity, you will need a photo of your face on a device or a large portrait of you, and a hand-held mirror, preferably square or rectangular. Your picture needs to have you facing straight on to the camera. Find the centre line down your face and hold the mirror on that line. When you hold the mirror to reflect the right side and then the left side, did you notice something different about your face? The images below show that there can be differences if you put two left-hand sides of your face together or if you put two right-hand sides of your face together.

Original Image	The two right sides joined	The two left sides joined

What did you notice about your face when you held the mirror up to the centre line?

____

Is your face symmetrical? ______________________________

Conduct some research to find out if humans like symmetrical faces or prefer non-symmetrical faces. What did you find out?

____

(5) Now connect this idea to the animal world. Are animal faces symmetrical? Conduct some research to find the answer.

____

____

TARGETING GENERAL CAPABILITIES: CRITICAL THINKING AND ETHICAL UNDERSTANDING YEARS 3–4 © PASCAL PRESS ISBN: 978-1925726-244

Consider alternatives

6 Can you make something that is unpopular, popular? One vegetable that many people do not like is brussels sprouts. Do you like them? Your task is to persuade people to eat more brussels sprouts. To start with, you need to brainstorm all the positive things about eating them and find some recipes using brussels sprouts. From the information you have found, write a persuasive paragraph to convince your friends or family to eat brussels sprouts.

7 How effective is your argument? To test your persuasive skills and to have people consider the benefits of eating brussels sprouts, you need to read your argument to friends or family to test how persuasive you are. Alternatively, you may want to film yourself delivering your argument using a device and put yourself in the location of the kitchen or even in the vegetable aisle of your supermarket.

8 How effective were you? Did you persuade anyone to eat more brussels sprouts? Record your answers below.

Seek solutions and put ideas into action

9 On page 10, you were asked to argue that messy bedrooms can sometimes be okay. However, there are times when you need to have a tidy bedroom. Your task is to help children who have messy bedrooms. Design a solution for storage, but to be environmentally aware, you have to use 5 items from recycling.
You are allowed to choose items from the school recycling area. Choose items from the table below that you could use in your design for a storage unit. You can use glue, a hammer and nails for your design.

empty plastic bottles	empty cardboard boxes	empty soda cans	used string from parcels	used shopping bags – plastic and material	rolled-up newspapers	large, empty Milo cans	student trays from old desks
2 crates	plastic garden ties	a small, old wheelie bin	3 old chairs	2 rolls of bubble wrap	one old whiteboard on wheels	2 old doors	2 old student desks

10 Draw and label your design for your storage device in this box or on a larger piece of paper.

Reflecting on thinking & processes – Unit 3

Brave Thinking

This unit asked you to think about your thinking! The big word to describe this is metacognition (met-a-cog-ni-tion) but we call it 'brave thinking'. Sometimes you have to change your thinking if it is stopping you from doing something you really want to do but are scared to try.

Think about thinking (metacognition)

The term 'living thing' refers to things that are now or once were alive. A non-living thing is anything that was never alive.

You have probably been learning about living and non-living things at school. Read the following information from the blog, *Kids Know Stuff*. This information will help you answer questions 2 and 3.

> All things in the world can be classified into living and non-living. Things that can breathe, eat, grow, move from one place to another, have feelings, reproduce their young ones and can die, are living things. For example, animals, insects, plants and human beings. If something obeys a few of the rules, it cannot be categorised as a living thing. It has to follow all the given rules very strictly. For example, an icicle, although it grows (increases in size), it is still a non-living thing since it cannot reproduce or breathe.
>
> Non-living things cannot do any of those actions. For example, balloons, see-saws, furniture and kites.

Fill in the table below with what you know about living and non-living things. Some information has already been filled in for you.

Living Things	Non-Living Things
	do not breathe
eat	
	do not have feelings
grow	

After thinking about what makes something living and non-living, provide three examples each of living and non-living things. Remember that living things have to obey all the rules.

	Living	Non-Living
Example 1		
Example 2		
Example 3		

We know that kites, balloons and see-saws are non-living things, but they all move. Can you explain why they are described as non-living? Use the space below to record your answer.

____

____

TARGETING GENERAL CAPABILITIES: CRITICAL THINKING AND ETHICAL UNDERSTANDING YEARS 3–4 © PASCAL PRESS ISBN: 978-1925726-244

Reflect on processes and transfer knowledge into new contexts

Dancing raisins

On page 21, you had to think like a scientist or inventor. In this assessment, you are once again going to use the PEMOE table to conduct a science investigation. Behaving like a scientist, you are going to put raisins/sultanas into a clear container of clear soda, such as lemonade or soda water. Use the table below to record your thinking.

My science investigation
Step 1 Predict Write or draw all the things you think will happen when you add raisins to a glass of soda.
Step 2 Explain Write the reasons why you think it will happen this way.
Step 3 Conduct the investigation Instructions: • Pour clear soda (lemonade or soda water) into a clear jar or glass. • Add some raisins one at a time.
Observe Draw or describe what you see when you add the raisins.
Explain (why it happened) To discover more about why the raisins danced, enter 'Dancing raisins experiment' in your web browser.

Source: Adapted from POE, developed by White and Gunstone (1992)

Analysing, synthesising & evaluating reasoning & procedures – Unit 4

Thinking and acting like a HERO

In this unit, you were asked to think like a hero. You were asked to think creatively and critically, and use your reasoning skills. You also learnt that looking is not always seeing. To be able to make reasonable decisions, you need to see the whole picture and make sure you have all the information. You also need to be aware that there are different points of view or perspectives that you need to consider before making a decision.

Apply logic and reasoning / Draw conclusions and design a course of action

1 A group of paintings has been discovered while cleaning out an old building. No-one is sure where they come from, so they have called you in as an Art Investigator to try and unravel the mystery. View the drawings below and write down five things you immediately notice about them with your art investigating training.

1. ______________________________
2. ______________________________
3. ______________________________
4. ______________________________
5. ______________________________

Talia

Sierra

Josh

Joseph

Breanna

Adele

Our grateful thanks for these wonderful illustrations supplied courtesy of Grange Primary Junior Class.

To help you go deeper into your investigation, have another look at the drawings and answer the following questions in the table below.

	QUESTIONS	ANSWERS
1	Who drew the pictures and how can you tell?	
2	What clues in the artwork tell you about what the children in the pictures were doing?	
3	How are the six pictures alike? List three ways they are alike.	1. 2. 3.
4	In what ways are the six pictures different from each other? List three things you notice.	1. 2. 3.

3 Artists use a variety of different techniques to create their artwork. These include: use of colour, shape, design, pattern, perspective and much more. The young artists who drew these pictures used many of those art techniques, including drawing themselves from different perspectives. Look at the paintings again. Where could you be standing or looking from (your perspective or point of view) to see the different paintings? Complete the table below by ticking the perspectives for each set of paintings. Discuss your choices with an adult.

The paintings	Looking down from above the pool	Looking up from the bottom of the pool	Looking from the side of the pool	Looking from the corner of the pool
Talia				
Sierra				
Josh and Joseph				
Adele and Breannah				

It is your turn to draw a picture of yourself swimming in a pool. Choose one or more of the perspectives listed in the table to make your drawing more interesting.

Evaluate procedures and outcomes

5 Looking is not always seeing. How much do you notice about the things that are around you every day? Before you make a decision about what you see, hear or read, you need to make sure you have all the correct information. Answer these questions about your home and then check your accuracy.

How many windows in your house, inside and out? ____________________

How many doors? ____________________

What side does your fridge door open, to the left or right? ____________________

If you are moving from inside to outside, which way does your sliding door move, to the left or to the right? ____________________

How many things are on the wall in your lounge room? ____________________

What is the number plate of your family car? ____________________

6 See how well your family pays attention to the things around the home. Ask them the same questions and work out who looks and actually sees the most.

Ethical Understanding

Through developing Ethical Understanding Capability, children learn to identify and investigate the nature of ethical concepts, values and character traits, and understand how reasoning can assist ethical judgement. As outlined in the curriculum, the elements and sub-elements are:

Understanding ethical concepts and issues — recognise ethical concepts; explore ethical concepts in context

Reasoning in decision-making and actions — reason and make ethical decisions; consider consequences; reflect on ethical action

Exploring values, rights and responsibilities — examine values; explore rights and responsibilities; consider points of view

English – Literacy, Literature & Language

Australian Curriculum Links: *Year 3 ACELY1678, ACELY1680, ACELT1596, ACELA1477 / Year 4 ACELY1691, ACELY1692, ACELT1603, ACELA1489*

Source: www.ethicsfun.com

Is it fair and inclusive?

Some students enjoy and are good at running around the oval while others may find it more difficult. Some students enjoy and are good at reading and writing and other schoolwork while others may find that more difficult. The way your friends and teachers support you, can help you get through difficult situations and be successful.

Examine the cartoon and answer the following questions.

 Who is the cartoon aimed at?

a) teachers

b) students who are good at sport

c) students who are not good at sport

d) all of the above

 Why does the teacher want everyone to do the cross-country run?

a) as a way for the class to bond

b) so Brett can win

c) for everyone to have fun

d) both a and c

 All the children were happy to be involved in the cross-country run.

True False

Explain why you answered the way you did.

____

____

____

 Everyone finished the run.

True False

 Everyone finished the run at the same time.

True False

Understanding ethical concepts & issues

6. Do you think everyone enjoyed the cross-country run as the teacher said? Why or why not?

____

____

____

7. Explain why you think Brett has a smug face.

____

____

____

8. What could the teacher and students have done to support all students to have fun on the cross-country run?

____

____

____

9. Has there ever been a time when there was something you wanted to do but you were not included, or you felt things were not fair? Perhaps you were not picked for a team or left out of a game. Describe what happened, how you felt and what you did about it.

____

____

____

10. Have you heard of Kid President? In one of his videos he gives a pep talk about being awesome, believing in yourself and being fair to all. As he says, 'We were made to be awesome! Let's get out there!'

How are you awesome? Share your AWESOMENESS by listing three ways you are awesome.

1	2	3

TARGETING GENERAL CAPABILITIES: CRITICAL THINKING AND ETHICAL UNDERSTANDING YEARS 3–4 © PASCAL PRESS ISBN: 978-1925726-244

HASS – Inquiry and Skills

Australian Curriculum Links: *Year 3 ACHASSI054 / Year 4 ACHASSI075*

Is it fair? – Recognising ethical concepts

At school, everyone learns about fairness and justice, and may have class rules which help everyone feel included. What if one of your class rules is that if you give out party invitations at school, every class member gets an invitation?

Your friend, Mai, tells you that she doesn't want to invite three classmates to her party because they are often not very nice to her. Mai tells you about her plan to give everybody a map and instructions to the park where she is having the party. However, she wants to change the instructions on the maps for the three classmates she doesn't want to come. She hopes that they won't actually find the park and will miss out on the party. She asks you to help her write the wrong instructions on the map, and you agree.

Look at this Community Map, there are symbols on the side to tell you what the pictures represent. This is called a key. As you can see, there are two parks in the community. Mia's party will be held in the larger park, nearest the roundabout. The map has instructions to guide people to the party. The second box is for you to add instructions which will lead the students Mia doesn't want at her party to the other smaller park.

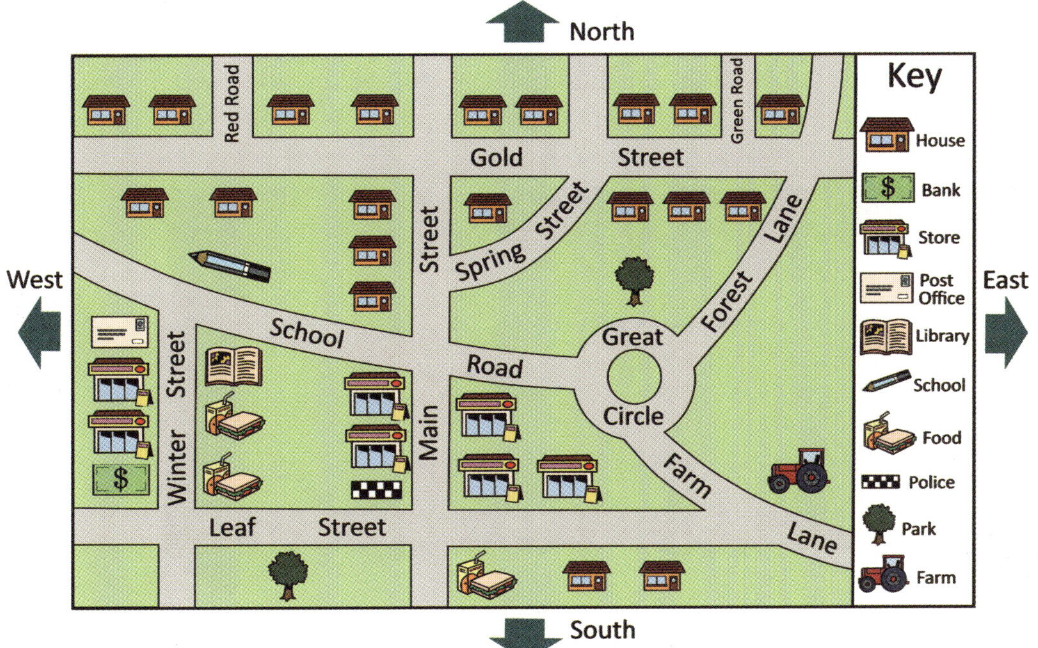

INSTRUCTIONS	INSTRUCTIONS
1. Start at the school as everyone knows where the school is.	1. Start at the school as everyone knows where the school is.
2. Turn left onto School Road, heading East.	2.
3. Continue past Main Street until you get to the Great Circle.	3.
4. Turn left onto the Great Circle, heading North.	4.
5. You will see the park on your left.	5.

TARGETING GENERAL CAPABILITIES: CRITICAL THINKING AND ETHICAL UNDERSTANDING YEARS 3–4 © PASCAL PRESS ISBN: 978-1925726-244

After you have helped Mia, you start to think how you would feel if someone did that to you. Answer the questions below.

i. Mia's party is a pretend activity, but what would you do if a friend really asked you to write the wrong instructions?

____

ii. How would you feel knowing you helped to send three classmates to the wrong park?

____

iii. What other solutions could Mia have used other than being unfair?

____

iv. What if you were one of the three students left out? How would you feel?

____

One sunny day, you find an old strange-looking map in one of the draws in the kitchen. It is a map you have never seen before, and it looks very much like a treasure map that pirates use. Imagine the treasure you could find buried under the large X. In pirate maps, X marks the spot where the treasure is buried.

Imagine you are a pirate! Draw an island on the map below. Draw lots of places on the island. Then draw an 'X' to show where your treasure is. Write directions to find your treasure!

Where is this treasure buried?

Directions

____

____

4. You may have seen movies about pirates and noticed that not all pirate captains behave the same way. Pirates had rules or a code that they followed, written by the pirate captain of the ship. If you were a pirate captain what would your name be? What rules or code would you write for your crew?

Your Name ______________________

Your Code ______________________

English – Literature

Australian Curriculum Links: *Year 3 ACELT1596 / Year 4 ACELT1603*

Being kind to be fair

1 Read the cartoon.

In your own words, describe what you think the cartoon is about.

____

____

____

Source: www.ethicsfun.com

Re-read the cartoon carefully and complete this table. The answers are in the text.

Reasons why the new kid was left out	Reasons why the new kid was included

Understanding ethical concepts & issues

3. Imagine what it would feel like to be the new kid at school. Write down three words that would describe the feeling.

   i. ____________ ii. ____________ iii. ____________

4. Think about a time when you treated someone differently because you did not want to include them in your game or activity. Use the sentence starters below to explain what happened.

   The person or people that I excluded was/were: ____________

   The reason I did this was: ____________

   The way I excluded them was: ____________

   This is what happened because I excluded them: ____________

   ____

5. Think about a time when you included someone because you thought about how they might be feeling in a particular situation. Explain:

   The person or people that I included was/were: ____________

   The reason I did this was: ____________

   The way I included them was: ____________

   This is what happened because I included them:

   ____

6. Did you know that children even younger than you, are forced to work like adults to earn money to support their families? Child labour is not casual work that you do to help out your family. These children often have their rights to education, protection, a safe home and enough food to eat taken away from them. They have lots of responsibilities but very few rights. Their work is often dangerous and harmful to their health. Some children work making bricks, on farms and in factories often making the clothing that we buy cheaply in Australia.

   Imagine that you are one of the children forced into child labour. Because your family is so poor, you have been forced to work in a factory that makes bricks. You work 6 days a week, 12 hours every day. It is hot, dangerous and very tiring work for anyone, let alone a child. Below are some of the things that might happen to you. Think about how you would feel and discuss this with an adult.

   - Working as a child labourer means you can no longer go to school.
   - The factory is a long way from your home in a place where you do not know anyone.
   - After working 12 hours a day you are too tired to even think about playing or having any fun.
   - You are often hungry as there is very little food and some of it is not fit to eat.

   Which one of these things do you think is the worst?

   ____

   ____

English – Language

Australian Curriculum Links: *Year 3 ACELA1476 / Year 4 ACELA1489*

Health and Physical Education – Personal, Social and Community Health

Australian Curriculum Links: *Years 3 & 4 ACPPS033, ACPPS037*

Reasoning – Fact or Opinion?

To make good decisions or use good reasoning, you need to understand the difference between opinions and facts.

An opinion is what you think about something. It can be your feelings or how someone else feels about something.

Facts are different from opinions because facts are always true and can be proven. Facts are about something that has really happened.

Look at the table below and work out which statements are fact and which ones are opinion.

Statement	Fact or Opinion?
A rainbow is more beautiful than a sunset.	
There are 26 letters in the alphabet.	
Not all birds can fly.	
Cats are easier to care for than dogs.	

Now it's your turn. Write two statements that are facts and two statements that are opinions about the topics provided.

Topics	Fact	Opinion
Visiting the doctor		
Doing homework		

Read the cartoon about Justin, Sanjay and friends, playing in a cricket team.

In the cartoon, Justin finally became successful in his cricket team. However, Justin could have been out of the team because of someone making a decision based on their opinion, without considering all the facts.

Source: www.ethicsfun.com

TARGETING GENERAL CAPABILITIES: CRITICAL THINKING AND ETHICAL UNDERSTANDING YEARS 3–4 © PASCAL PRESS ISBN: 978-1925726-244

Reasoning in decision-making & actions

3. The cartoon has conversations between people in the story. Some of the conversations include facts and some include opinions. Fill out the table below to work out which sentences are factual and which ones are an opinion, and explain your reasons.

Text	Fact or opinion?	Reasoning — Explain your reasons
We lost AGAIN Sanjay,		
because Justin can't bat.		
He shouldn't be in the team.		
I think he just gets nervous during a game.		
I have seen him bat really well in the playground.		
It was awful. We might have won if I had played better.		
Out for a duck. AGAIN!		
I thought you might like to do some cricket practice.		
I have a spare bat.		
Really? I was thinking of quitting. But more practice might help.		
Great shot Justin!		

Source: www.ethicsfun.com

TARGETING GENERAL CAPABILITIES: CRITICAL THINKING AND ETHICAL UNDERSTANDING YEARS 3–4 © PASCAL PRESS ISBN: 978-1925726-244

 Look at the frames taken from the original cartoon. Which statement shows how Justin was feeling about himself?

When Justin got out for a duck ...

a) he was happy because he thought he played well.

b) he blamed the team for losing.

c) he thought it was because his mum didn't come to the game.

d) he thought he could have played better.

 Look closely at the last frame of the cartoon. Find three things in the cartoon that give you an idea of how Justin was feeling. One example has been done for you. How do you think Justin was feeling?

How Justin was feeling	What you saw in the cartoon
Justin felt relieved that he did not get out for a duck.	Justin has a big smile on his face.

 Everyone has opinions about lots of things, and sometimes they also know facts about the topic. Check back to question 1 to remind yourself of the difference between a fact and an opinion.

Sort out the facts from the opinions relating to the topics in the table below.

The Topics	Information	Fact or Opinion?
Bananas	Bananas float in water.	
	To whiten teeth naturally, you can rub the inside of a banana peel on your teeth for two minutes every night.	
	I think bananas grow on trees.	
	The only way to eat a banana split is with strawberry ice-cream.	
Elephant	Elephants are afraid of bees.	
	Elephants don't like peanuts.	
	Elephants can get sunburned.	
	A good food for elephants is peanuts.	
Hair	I prefer red hair to blonde hair.	
	My hair grows faster in winter than in summer.	
	Pigeon poo can be used to dye hair blonde.	
	Humans have the same amount of hair follicles as chimpanzees.	

English – Literacy & Literature

Australian Curriculum Links: *Year 3 ACELY1675 / Year 4 ACELT1607, ACELT1794*

Mathematics – Statistics and Probability

Australian Curriculum Links: *Year 3 ACMSP069, ACMSP070 / Year 4 ACMSP095, ACMSP096*

Reasoning – Fair or not fair?

The story of Little Red Riding Hood is about a little girl who wears a red cape that has a hood. One day, when she is walking through the woods on her way to visit her granny, she meets a wolf! To find out what happens next, complete the story below by filling in the missing words and phrases. A list of possible answers is below the story.

LITTLE RED RIDING HOOD – A VERY SHORT STORY!

'Hello!' said the wolf. 'Where are you going?'

'I'm going to see my granny. She lives in the cottage in the middle of the woods,' __________ Little Red Riding Hood.

'What's in your basket?' asked the wolf.

Little Red Riding Hood told the wolf, 'My mum has baked a nice __________ for my granny. I am taking it to Granny __________ she is sick in bed.'

The wolf smiled __________ and quickly ran to Granny's house.

He had a __________.

When Little Red Riding Hood arrived at Granny's house, she called out, 'Hello Granny, I __________ you a nice cake!'

She then heard a very strange voice call out to her, 'I am in bed so bring me the cake, I want to EA ... I mean, see you.'

As she looked at Granny __________ in the bed, Little Red Riding Hood said, 'Granny, what big eyes you have!'

'All the better to see you with,' was the reply.

'But Granny, what a big nose you have!'

'All the better to __________ you with,' was the reply.

'But Granny, what big teeth you have!'

'All the better to EAT ...'

Possible Answers

cake	brought	smell	slyly
because	replied	lying	plan

TARGETING GENERAL CAPABILITIES: CRITICAL THINKING AND ETHICAL UNDERSTANDING YEARS 3–4 © PASCAL PRESS ISBN: 978-1925726-244

2. The ending of this story depends on you. Write three different endings to the story in the table below. Use the information in the top row of the table to help you decide what will happen next.

If you would like to see a different version, you can view this story from Roald Dhal: https://www.youtube.com/watch?v=Pq161aoLQ1A.

The wolf was very hungry, so what happens next?	Granny is alive and baking cakes in the kitchen, so what happens next?	Little Red Riding Hood is an expert in kung fu and boxing, so what happens next?
'All the better to EAT ...	'All the better to EAT ...	'All the better to EAT ...

3. Was the wolf doing the wrong thing or was he just being a wolf? What do wolves eat? According to the story, the wolf wanted to eat Little Red Riding Hood, and because of this, he has often been called, 'The Big Bad Wolf'. Does he deserve this title? Go to this site and find out what wolves eat: https://kids.kiddle.co/Wolf.

I found out wolves eat ______________________________.

4. You would have found out that wolves are carnivores or meat eaters. Now, Little Red Riding Hood was in the wolf's home area or habitat and she is also made of meat. If the wolf was hungry, should he have eaten or tried to eat Little Red Riding Hood? Is he in the wrong? Is it fair to call him 'The Big Bad Wolf'?

One way to find out what people think about this is to conduct a survey. This could also help you decide.

Collect the answers of up to 10 of your classmates or your family and friends.

Should the wolf in the story, *Little Red Riding Hood*, be called 'The Big Bad Wolf'?

Who you asked	Yes, and reasons for their answer	No, and reasons for their answer	Maybe and reasons why

Reasoning in decision-making & actions

5 Make a bar graph using the graph outline below to show how many people answered yes, no or maybe. Have a look at the example of a bar graph to help you display your information.

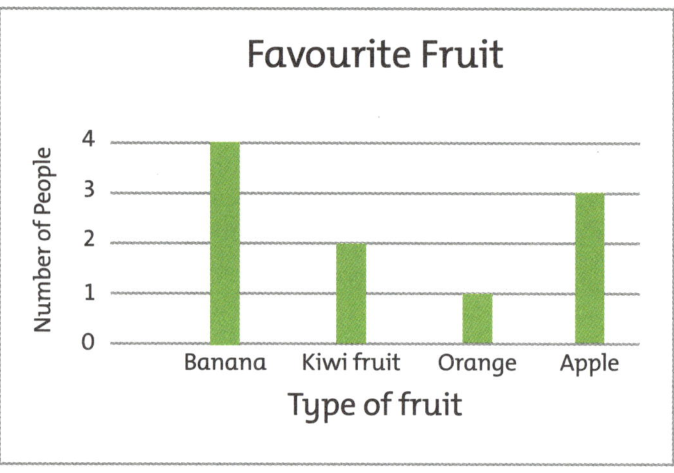

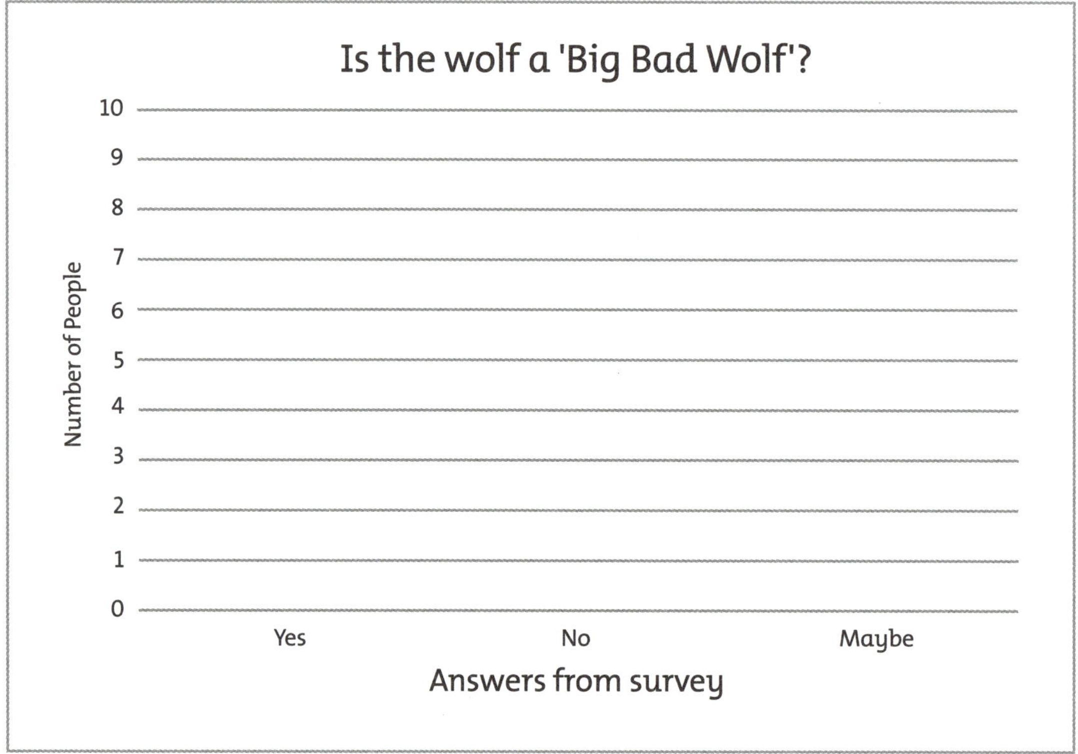

6 The wolf's side of the story.

If the wolf had to defend himself and try to persuade people that he is not bad but just being a wolf, what would he say? Help the wolf by filling in his speech bubble.

TARGETING GENERAL CAPABILITIES: CRITICAL THINKING AND ETHICAL UNDERSTANDING YEARS 3–4 © PASCAL PRESS ISBN: 978-1925726-244

English – Literature & Literacy

Australian Curriculum Links: *Year 3 ACELT1596, ACELY1675, ACELY1677 / Year 4 ACELT1603, ACELY1689*

Health and Physical Education – Personal, Social and Community Health

Australian Curriculum Links: *Years 3 & 4 ACPPS036*

Good choices and bad choices – Choosing honesty!

 Read the cartoon and complete the table below.

i. What did Brett want to do with the money he found?	
ii. What did Lucy want Brett to do with the money?	
iii. Why did Brett want to return the money?	
iv. Why did Lucy think it was okay to keep the money?	

 Who do you think was making the right choice? Circle your answer.
Brett Lucy

 Re-read the cartoon and give reasons for your answer.

____

____

4. How would you feel if, like the little girl, you had lost the money for an excursion to the zoo? You can choose more than one answer. Discuss your answers with an adult.
   a) You would not care as your parents would give you more.
   b) You would feel anxious and worried that you would get into trouble.
   c) You would feel relieved because you did not want to go on the excursion anyway.
   d) You would feel angry at yourself for losing the money.

5. Describe how you would feel if someone had found and returned the money to you.

____

____

6. In the cartoon, Brett chose to be honest and return the money to the office. He made this choice even though Lucy wanted him to keep the money so they could spend it.

Who
What
When
Where
How
Why
?

Think about a time when you have made an honest choice even though it was hard to do.

Fill in the table below to explain what happened, using the 5Ws + H strategy.

Look at the example to guide your answer.

5 Ws + HE

Who	What	When	Why	Where	HOW did you feel about what had happened?	EXPLAIN what you chose to do and why
me	I dropped the iPad and broke the screen.	in the first lesson in the morning	I was being silly and tried to throw it up and catch it.	in the classroom	I felt stupid that I had broken it, and I felt scared that I was going to get in trouble.	I showed the teacher the broken screen and told her what I had done. I owned up because I didn't want anyone else to get in trouble for my silliness.

Your turn

Who	What	When	Why	Where	HOW did you feel about what had happened?	EXPLAIN what you chose to do and why

TARGETING GENERAL CAPABILITIES: CRITICAL THINKING AND ETHICAL UNDERSTANDING YEARS 3–4 © PASCAL PRESS ISBN: 978-1925726-244

Mathematics – Number and Algebra

Australian Curriculum Links: *Year 3 ACMNA059 / Year 4 ACMNA080*

English – Literacy & Language

Australian Curriculum Links: *Year 3 ACELY1675, ACELA1476 / Year 4 ACELY1688, ACELA1488*

The BBQ

You have been invited to a BBQ at your friend's home. Your friend's house is next door to a shop. You and your friend are allowed to go into the shop and buy enough food to feed 8 people at the BBQ: 4 children and 4 adults. You have been given $20 and asked to buy 4 things for the BBQ. Help your friend decide which items they can buy for $20 or less.

When you get to the store, you see that on the special's board are some of the things you have been asked to buy. Read the specials board.

1. Make a shopping list of what items you will buy and add up their cost to make sure that you do not go over the $20.

Items bought	Cost	Reasons for choosing the item
TOTAL COST		

Exploring values, rights & responsibilities

2 Early debating

Your friend was given $20 to go to the shop to purchase things for the family BBQ. When you both arrived at the store, you found that many items were on special. After purchasing the 4 items, you had $3.25 left out of the $20 you were given. What will you do with the change?

Your friend's mother would not know that there would be change from the $20. Complete the chart below by circling YES or NO to each statement and explain why you have chosen your answer. What else should your friend do? Add another action in the last space.

What should your friend do?	Yes or no?	Your reasons why
Should your friend spend the $3.25 on something for themselves?	YES / NO	
Should your friend spend the $3.25 on something for the family?	YES / NO	
Should your friend spend the $3.25 on something to share with you?	YES / NO	
Should your friend give back the $3.25 change to their mother?	YES / NO	

3 You are saving up to buy something you have always wanted. To help you save money, your parents have decided to pay you pocket money for one week if you do jobs around the house to help them. The jobs you need to do around the house include:

- setting the table each night
- packing and unpacking the dishwasher or helping dry the dishes
- putting the bins out
- helping walk the dog and feeding the pets
- cleaning your bedroom and making your bed every day
- cleaning your teeth twice a day
- going to bed straightaway when they tell you to
- packing and unpacking your school bag each day.

Can you think of two more jobs you could do to help your parents? Record them below.

____

____

4 Your parents ask you to make a decision. They will either:

i. pay you $10 a day for one week

ii. pay you $1 for the first day and then double your pocket money every day for a week.

Without working it out, what is your first choice, i or ii? ________

Why did you choose this option?

____

TARGETING GENERAL CAPABILITIES: CRITICAL THINKING AND ETHICAL UNDERSTANDING YEARS 3–4 © PASCAL PRESS ISBN: 978-1925726-244

 Use the table below to help you work out how much you will get at the end of the week.

DAY	ADD $10 A DAY	DOUBLE PAYMENT EACH DAY
1	$10	$1
2	$20	$2
3		
4		
5		
6		
7		
TOTAL		

 After working out the different totals, will you change your mind on your first decision?_______________

Why or why not?

____

 Your parents lost track of the days. How much would you get if they paid you for 8 days?

DAY	ADD $10 A DAY	DOUBLE PAYMENT EACH DAY
8		

 Now that you have all this information, what agreement would you like to make with your parents?

a) Work for 7 days and be paid $10 a day.
b) Work for 7 days and have the payments double each day.
c) Work for 8 days and be paid $10 a day.
d) Work for 8 days and have the payments double each day.
e) Work for free.

 Why did you choose your answer?

____

(10) If you had worked 7 days but your parents lost track of time and paid you for 8 days, what would you do? Choose one or more answers from the ones provided. You would ...

a) not say anything and keep the money.
b) not say anything and work an extra week, keeping the money.
c) tell them and give back the extra money.
d) tell them and keep the money as a reward for honesty.
e) negotiate another agreement for the next week.

(11) Why did you choose your answer/s?

____

____

Exploring values, rights & responsibilities

HASS – Civics and Citizenship

Australian Curriculum Links: *Year 3 ACHASSK071, ACHASSK072 / Year 4 ACHASSK091*

ETHICAL UNDERSTANDING

Rights and responsibility

1. You have just received a new iPad. You want to use it right away; however, you are told that you have to come up with a plan on how to use it safely. But what does that mean? Does it mean:
   - when to use it?
   - how to use it?
   - sites and web addresses you are allowed to go on?
   - the amount of time spent on using it?
   - where you are allowed to take it?

   To help you come up with a plan:
   - ask your friends what their rules are in using their devices
   - ask your family and other trusted adults what they think the rules of use of your iPad should be.

   To help you, write down what you have found out in the table below.

2. Using this information, design a contract that you will sign in front of your parents. The contract is about how you will safely use your device and it has to have your parents' approval.

3. All children have rights, and along with these rights come responsibilities that children must understand. One of your responsibilities is to take care of your things and be grateful for what you have. In the table below are some of your rights. You need to work out your responsibilities for each right. How would you take care of each one and show gratitude for what you have? Add to the list of responsibilities already in the table.

You have a right to:	You have a responsibility to:
i. live in a safe, warm and clean home	• keep your room tidy and clean •
ii. have enough food to eat	• not to waste any food •
iii. have clothes to wear that keep you warm and dry	• help with the laundry •

TARGETING GENERAL CAPABILITIES: CRITICAL THINKING AND ETHICAL UNDERSTANDING YEARS 3–4 © PASCAL PRESS ISBN: 978-1925726-244

Understanding ethical concepts & issues – Unit 5

Is it fair and inclusive?

In this unit, you worked on activities that made you think about being fair and including others in your games or activities. You worked on tasks that showed how important it is to feel that you belong to a family or group of friends and how being kind in your actions can also mean you are being fair and inclusive.

Recognise ethical concepts / Explore ethical concepts in context

The day that you and your classmates have been practising for has finally arrived. It is the day where teams of students compete against each other in games and activities—the school Sports Day. It is a very special day because you are the House Captain of your team in the school Sports Day.

You have a very difficult job ahead of you because you have to select 2 people for each of the novelty events.

Many of the students in your house team have already competed in the track and field events, such as relays and long jump. The problem is that there are 8 students who are keen to participate in the novelty events, but you know they are not very athletic, and they have not been involved in any event so far.

If you win three of the novelty events, your house team will be the overall winner for the Sports Day. So, who will you pick? You need 10 people to fill the places available.

What are you going to do and why?

Novelty Events	8 students who have not participated yet and are not very athletic		4 students who are very good athletes and who have already participated
• wheelbarrow race	• Annabel	• Eli	• Ian
• egg and spoon race	• Byron	• Fran	• Juanita
• three-legged race	• Caleb	• Gita	• Kurt
• sack race	• Danuta	• Han	• Luane
• water bucket relay			

Complete this table to show your thinking.

Novelty Race	Who will you pick to compete?		Why did you choose these students?
wheelbarrow race			
egg and spoon race			
three-legged race			
sack race			
water bucket relay			

While on your way home from the sports day, you find an envelope with a message and a map. The message reads:

> To Billy the Kid from Gangster Granny.
>
> Billy, I have a map to show where I buried the treasure. I buried it in the park, but you need to dig it up when it is safe to do so. I have to leave town to attend a retirement party. Take the treasure and see if you can make use of it. Any money you make from the treasure, you need to remember that half of it is mine!!!!!!
>
> I have written instructions next to the map.

Read the instructions and mark on the map where the X would be.

i. Head to the park in the dark. Don't go to the East or West side, no good places to hide.
ii. Tiptoe through the tulips to find the garden path.
iii. Leave the path where you see children going up and down. A donkey's sound rhymes with this equipment.
iv. Head towards something from the beach, but it is not the beach.
v. Turn South to find some slippery children.
vi. You may hear some quackers but ignore the noise.
vii. Find something that rhymes with 'flea'.
viii. Go to the 'flea' closest to where children sing (missing letter).
ix. Place an X at the West side of the 'flea'.
x. This is where the treasure is!
xi. Start digging!

After you have marked where the treasure is located, what will you do? Explain what you would do next and why.

____

____

____

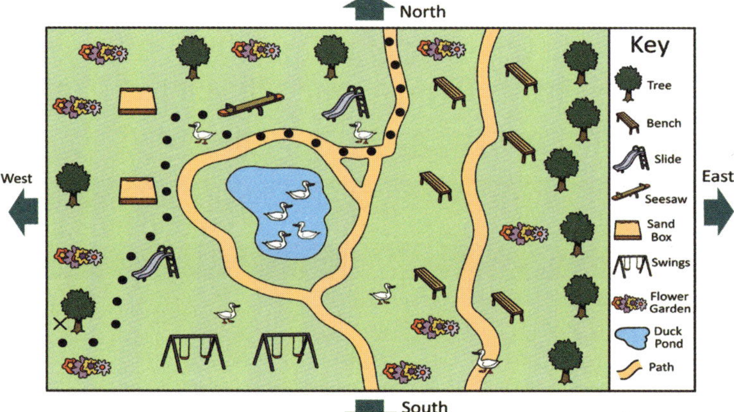

Here are some maps that children drew of the route that they travel from home to school. You will notice that each child drew and labelled on their maps places that are important to them or that stand out on the way to school.

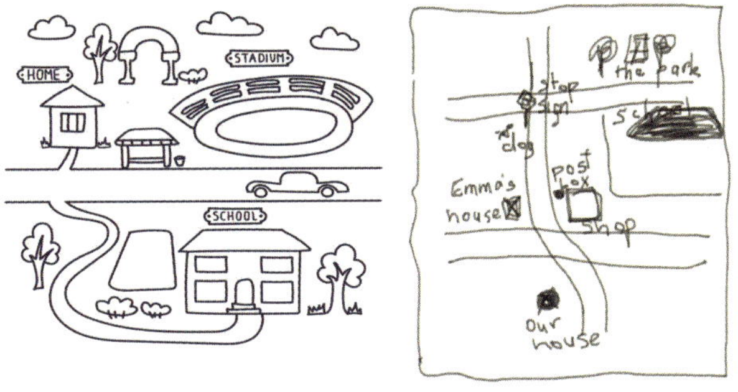

Draw a map of the way you travel from home to school. Put on your map anything that you think is important and label it.

If you had to hide something, like treasure, what would it be and where would you hide it? Mark an X on your map where you would hide something. Explain why you chose that spot and what 'treasure' you would hide!

____

____

TARGETING GENERAL CAPABILITIES: CRITICAL THINKING AND ETHICAL UNDERSTANDING YEARS 3–4 © PASCAL PRESS ISBN: 978-1925726-244

Reasoning in decision-making & actions – Unit 6

Reasoning – Fact or Opinion?

In this unit, you explored the difference between fact and opinion, and you saw that making decisions or taking action without all of the facts can end up causing problems.

If you act just on opinions, without all the facts, you can end up acting very unfairly towards someone. In the story of Little Red Riding Hood, the wolf could think that he was unfairly described as 'The Big Bad Wolf'.

Reason and make ethical decisions / Consider consequences / Reflect on ethical action

Your reasoning and decision-making skills are needed to sort out the facts from the opinions to make sure that there are not unintended harmful consequences, for example, to stop someone being unfairly accused of stealing.

Read the School of the Woods Newsletter below. Underline any information you read that will help you understand what has happened.

SCHOOL OF THE WOODS, NEWSLETTER – TERM 2, WEEK 5

MYSTERY SURROUNDS MISSING LUNCHES

Two students found no lunches in their bags when the lunch bell rang. They reported their missing lunches to the principal. If anyone can help solve the mystery, please contact the principal immediately. Principal Furrier said that he would be interviewing everyone who may have seen something to hopefully shed some light on the missing lunches.

SCHOOL UNIFORM SHOP

School of the Woods winter uniform is now available for sale. Contact Ms Mink (pictured here), for pricing and shop opening hours.

REMINDER

The school canteen will be closed in Week 5 this term due to maintenance. Please remember to provide lunch for your child/children.

COLD WEATHER WEAR

Due to the very cold weather we are currently having, it is good to see teachers and students have been dressing warmly when they are outdoors.

Principal Furrier interviewed a number of people and wrote down what they told him. Read each of the interview statements and:

a) use the 'Facts/Opinion' column to sort out the facts from the opinions. The first one has been done for you

b) look back at the facts you have underlined in the newsletter and underline any more information that you think will help you.

ASSESSMENT

PRINCIPAL FURRIER'S INTERVIEW NOTES

Persons interviewed	Interview statements	Facts	Opinions
Red Riding, a Year 4 student	Inya Hood and I came out to get our lunch out of our bags in the rack. Then we saw something big and hairy disappearing around the corner of the building near where our bags were! My mum makes nice lunches, and the kids ask me to share. I reckon someone stole it.	- came out to get our lunch out of our bags - saw something around the corner of the building	- It was big and hairy. - My mum makes nice lunches. - I reckon someone stole it.
Inya Hood, a Year 4 student	When Red Riding and I looked in our school bags, our lunches WERE NOT THERE! We think they had been STOLEN! I bet I know who!		
Mrs Lupin, a Year 3 teacher (pictured)	It was a very cold day, and I was on my way to do playground duty when the lunch bell rang. I wore my very warm coat as I was going outdoors. I don't think there was a big hairy thing although I did see my reflection in the window, ha ha!		
Ms Mink, the school Uniform Shop Manager (pictured)	I am surprised you are asking me. On that day, I was just on my way to open the uniform shop and if there was a big hairy thing, well I didn't see it. I did overhear two students talking. They may have said something about their lunches.		
Frannie Frizz, a Year 3 student (pictured)	My mum gave me money to buy my lunch at the canteen, but it was closed. I had to go to the office to get an emergency lunch. I don't like them. Inya and Red most likely thought I was the big hairy thing.		

After considering all the information and facts, read the possible solutions below. Circle one or more of the numbered solutions that you think could be possible. Write in the last column why you think the solutions are possible or not possible.

	SOLUTIONS	REASON WHY
1	Inya Hood and Red Riding's lunches were never stolen because they did not have them in their bags in the first place. They left them at home.	
2	Mrs Lupin was hungry, so she stole the girl's lunches as she was walking to do yard duty.	
3	The girls saw Frannie Frizz and believed that she took the girl's lunches out of their bags.	
4	Inya Hood and Red Riding were given money for lunches at the canteen. Their mother had not read the Newsletter saying the canteen was closed. The girls made up the story of the stolen lunches to keep the money.	
5	Ms Mink was the 'big hairy thing' the girls saw when they went to their bags. She was wearing her fur coat because it was a very cold day.	

What do you think really happened?

____

____

Exploring values, rights & responsibilities – Unit 7

Good choices and bad choices – Choosing honesty!

In this unit, we looked at the importance of making good choices instead of bad choices. To help us make good choices, we need to think about our values, rights and responsibilities and also those of other people in our community. As humans, we have to consider how our actions might affect others.

Examine values – Honesty

Stories that were written many years ago that teach children a moral or lesson are called fables. One fable is *The Shepherd Boy and the Wolf*.

A shepherd boy looked after a flock of sheep for his village near a dark forest, not far from the village. Soon he became bored.

One day, he thought of a plan to amuse himself. His uncle had told him to call for help should a wolf attack the flock, and the people in the village would chase it away. So now, though he had not seen anything that even looked like a wolf, he ran toward the village, shouting at the top of his voice, 'Wolf! Wolf!'

As he expected, the villagers who heard the cry dropped their work and ran quickly to the boy, but when they got there, they found the boy laughing at the trick he had played on them.

A few days later, the shepherd boy again shouted, 'Wolf! Wolf!' The villagers ran to help him, only to be laughed at again.

Then one evening, a wolf really did come from the forest and attack the sheep. In terror, the boy ran toward the village shouting, 'Wolf! Wolf!' Even though the villagers heard the cry, they did not run to help him as they had before. 'He cannot fool us again,' they said.

The wolf killed a great many of the boy's sheep and then slipped away into the forest.

A video that shows this story can be found at: https://www.youtube.com/watch?v=gKWktweAZb0.

1. What did the boy do that annoyed the villagers?
   a) He talked all the time.
   b) He did not guard the sheep at all.
   c) He tricked the villagers by calling out that there was a wolf.
   d) He was always late for work and left the sheep unprotected.

2. Why didn't the villagers run to help the shepherd boy the third time he called?

   ____

   ____

3. Would you have believed the shepherd boy the third time he shouted, 'Wolf'? Why or why not?

   ____

   ____

ASSESSMENT

Explore rights and responsibilities / Consider points of view

Imagine that you are lucky enough to have a park near your house that you use regularly with your family. One day, your family receives a note in the mail from the local council, letting residents know that the council is creating some off-leash areas in the park. This means that dog owners can let their dogs off the leash in certain areas of the park. Is this a good thing? Will this be fair to all people who use the park?

To help answer these questions, you need to think of the good points for this decision and also the negative points. Use the table below to list two ideas why it is a good idea and two ideas why it is not a good idea. An example has been provided to help you understand the task.

Why an off-leash area is a good idea	Why an off-leash area is not a good idea
People who like dogs but do not own one can go to an area to visit many dogs.	It will make the park smaller for other activities.

A local council member has volunteered to visit the park and answer any questions people have about the plan. You have a chance to ask the councillor some questions. From the list below, choose questions that you think will help you decide if the off-leash idea is good or not.

QUESTIONS	CHOOSE YES OR NO
How much of the park will be used for the off-leash section?	YES or NO
Will my dog behave itself in the park?	YES or NO
Will the off-leash section be fenced?	YES or NO
Would you be allowed in that section if you do not have a dog?	YES or NO
Will there be certain time restrictions as to when the off-leash part can be used?	YES or NO
What if I am scared of dogs?	YES or NO
Did you make this rule because you like dogs?	YES or NO

The councillor was very impressed with your questions, so they have asked you to help them write some rules for the area. You have been asked to write three rules to make sure that all people have equal use of the park.

Use the space below to write your rules. An example has been provided to help you understand the task.

RULES FOR THE FAIR USE OF THE PARK FOR EVERYONE

1 All areas of the park are available for everyone to use.

2

3

4

TARGETING GENERAL CAPABILITIES: CRITICAL THINKING AND ETHICAL UNDERSTANDING YEARS 3–4 © PASCAL PRESS ISBN: 978-1925726-244

CRITICAL & CREATIVE THINKING CAPABILITY

Unit 1

Pages 5-6: English – Literacy

1 Responses will vary.

2 Australia, Japan, China, Germany, Italy, France, Spain

3

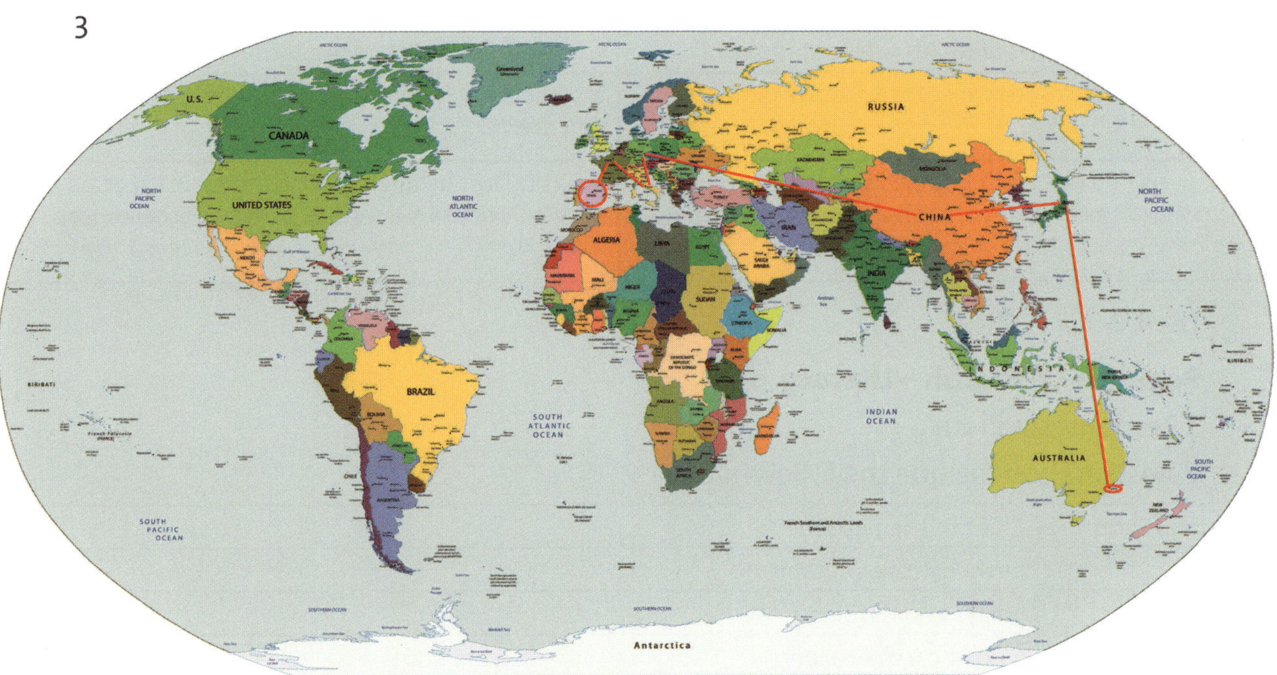

4 Morocco

Pages 7-9: HASS – Civics and Citizenship

1

Rule	Reason for the rule
1 Children should go to bed at ______________.	To get enough sleep for the next day. Children need more sleep than adults.
2 There may be specific hours of screen time, chores to do or a set homework time.	All these will help children with time management and to be healthy. Specific chores teach responsibility and how to contribute to the household.

2

	Rule	Possible consequence of no rule
	Hazardous materials should be locked away and are not to be touched by children.	Poisoning, accidental burning and/or irritation of skin and eyes. Some may be flammable.
	Computers and screens are visible to adults at all times. Screen time is limited, websites checked.	Inappropriate contacts and sites visited, online bullying, lack of sleep.
	Screen time is limited to certain hours of the day. Certain shows may be off limits.	Lack of sleep. Disturbed sleep due to inappropriate content watched.
	A sometimes food, so there are rules on how much and when.	Sugar overload and caffeine. Diabetes, poor dental health.
	A sometimes food, so there are rules on how much and when.	Sugar overload and caffeine. Diabetes, poor dental health.

3 Responses will vary.

4 Surname – Bushman, Given Names – Morgan, Nationality – Australian, Gender – male, Date of Birth – the date 21 years ago

5

	Rule	Consequences for not following the rule
1	Always keep your valuables safe and in sight.	They may be stolen as Morgan found out.
2	Always inform someone of your travel plans.	If something happens to you, people know where you are.
3	Always find out what you need to do before you arrive in a new country so that you are prepared.	You may not be allowed into the country or you may get into more serious trouble, like Morgan.

Unit 2

Pages 10-11: English – Literacy

1 Responses will vary.

2 Answers can include the following:

Activities/Food	Clues in the picture
cake	birthday cake on table
painting	paints and easel
exercise	weight on the carpet
pets	cat in the drawer and dog on the carpet, their bowls on the floor
chips	packet on the carpet
chess	board on carpet
sport	basketball, bowling pin, bike and pump
travel	stickers on the trunk
science	flask, microscope and spaceships, skull
music	instruments and metronome
pizza	box on the floor
peanuts	bag of peanuts on desk
ancient history	picture on wall and in bookcase, Viking helmet
cards	cards around the room
fish	starfish and fishbowl

3–5 Responses will vary.

Page 12: English – Language

1–2 Responses will vary.

Page: 13 Mathematics – Measurement and Geometry

1 Responses may vary but can include: Symmetry is when one half of an object is a mirror image of the other half.

2 Drawn images will look symmetrical.

3 Images will vary but should appear symmetrical.

TARGETING GENERAL CAPABILITIES: CRITICAL THINKING AND ETHICAL UNDERSTANDING YEARS 3–4 © PASCAL PRESS ISBN: 978-1925726-244

Pages 14-15: Technologies – Design and Technologies

1 Responses will vary but can include: A brick – a booster seat in the car/a bookend/a diving aid/a 'pet' brick; A fork – a pitchfork for a small farmer/a comb for small beards/ tied on a string and used as a Christmas ornament/ a back scratcher for small people; A toothbrush – an eyebrow brush/a broom for a mouse/a paintbrush for kids/heat the handle and curl it around to make a bracelet

3 Responses will vary and may include:

The objects are: 1 – two small funnels 2 – eye drops 3 – glasses	The objects are: 1 – two small umbrellas 2 – new shoes	The objects are: 1 __________ 2 __________
The problem is you have trouble putting drops into your own eyes.	The problem is expensive shoes getting wet in the rain.	The problem is ...
The drawing of your invention.	The drawing of your invention.	The drawing of your invention.

4–7 Responses will vary.

Unit 3

Pages 16-17: Health and Physical Education – Personal, Social and Community Health

1 Responses will vary.

2 They are in the kitchen because we can see a kettle and saucepans, kitchen cupboards and drawers, and a kitchen table.

3 c

4 d

5 Responses will vary.

6 Responses will vary but could include a–c.

Pages 18-19: The Arts – Visual / Technologies – Design and Technologies

1–3 Responses will vary.

Pages 20-21: Science – Chemical Understanding and Inquiry Skills

1 They were all invented or discovered by accident.

3 Responses will vary.

5 Responses will vary.

ANSWERS

Unit 4

Pages 22-24: English – Language & Literacy / HASS – Inquiry and Skills

1 Responses will vary but should include some of the Qualities of a hero and some Heroic Actions.

2 Responses will vary, depending on responses to question 1.

Pages 25-27: The Arts – Visual Arts / English – Language & Literacy

1 Responses will vary but could include: flowers, trees, ferns, skeleton of a bird, a deer, a glove and hat, a tent, writing, seed pods.

2 Responses will vary. 3 The picture shown is part of a mosaic picture of a seagull.

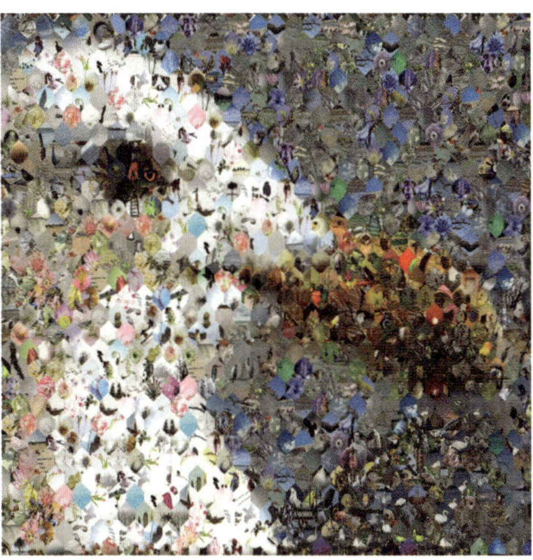

4 Drawings will vary but should be able to be identified as the parts described.

5 i. It is an elephant. ii. Responses will vary but there should be a clear link to the descriptions given in question 4.

6 The animal is an emu.

Clue 1	Clue 2	Clue 3	Clue 4	Answer
Its feathered side	Its beak.	Its legs	Its neck	An emu

7 Responses will vary.

8 Drawings may vary, but they should clearly show that they have been drawn from the three different perspectives.

9 Drawings will vary, but each shark and surfer character has a body of the observer, in this case, the emu. Check back to the book to see how the fish saw the other creatures.

10 Responses will vary depending on past experiences.

TARGETING GENERAL CAPABILITIES: CRITICAL THINKING AND ETHICAL UNDERSTANDING YEARS 3–4 © PASCAL PRESS ISBN: 978-1925726-244

CRITICAL AND CREATIVE THINKING ASSESSMENTS

Inquiring, exploring and organising information and ideas

Page 28: Pose questions / Identify and clarify information and ideas

1 Responses will vary.

Pages 28-29: Organise and process information

2 **Laws**: Do not litter./Stop at a red light./Do not steal./Stop at a stop sign./Walk across a road when the walk light is green.

Rules: Raise your hand to speak in class./Listen to your teacher./Clean up your room./ Walk in a line to your next lesson./Get along with others and no bullying at school.

3

	Question	Rule/Law	Who enforces it?	Consequences of breaking the rule/law
1	Drive at a reduced speed in school zones.	law	govt. & police	Fines or possible jail for repeat offences
2	Raise your hand to speak in class.	rule	teacher	Timeout, reminder
3	You must go to bed by 8:30 pm.	rule	parents	Be tired in the morning/lose privileges like playing games on your iPad
4	You must not steal from others.	law	govt. & police	Community service or even sent to jail
5	Tackling is not permitted.	rule	school – teachers/ club – coach	Sent off the oval/miss games/ banned from playing for the season or longer
6	No littering on beaches.	law	council	Fined and or do community service to pick up litter

Generating ideas, possibilities and actions

Page 30: Imagine possibilities and connect ideas

2 Our faces are symmetrical in that we have one eye, one ear, one eyebrow etc. on each side of our face. However, if we hold a mirror to the centre of our face, one side of our face is bigger than the other. When you put the mirror images of your face together, you will find that one side of your face is thinner than the other. It is rare to find a really symmetrical face.

3 Normally, your face is not symmetrical.

4 From research, there are varying answers; however, the majority of answers say that humans are attracted to symmetrical faces.

5 Like in humans, it is rare to have exactly symmetrical faces in animals.

Page 31: Consider alternatives

6–8 Responses will vary.

Page 31: Seek solutions and put ideas into action

9–10 Responses will vary; however, only five recycled items are to be used in the design.

Reflecting on thinking and processes

Page 32: Think about thinking (metacognition)

2 Living Things: breathe/eat/die/have feelings/move from one place to another/grow/produce their young

Non-Living Things: do not breathe/do not eat/do not die/do not have feelings/cannot move on their own/do not grow/cannot reproduce

3 Responses will vary; however, all living examples must follow all the given rules.

4 The kites, balloons and seesaws are non-living because they do not: breathe, eat, die, have feelings, grow or reproduce. They do move; however, they cannot move on their own.

Page 33: Reflect on processes and transfer knowledge into new contexts

5 Responses will vary in the steps of the PEMOE TABLE. The explanation is outlined in the video. The reason the raisins seem to 'dance' is that the bubbles of carbon dioxide in the soda attach themselves to the raisins and float them to the top of the glass. When the top is reached, the bubbles of carbon dioxide are released, and the raisins fall back to the bottom of the glass.

Analysing, synthesising and evaluating reasoning and procedures

Pages 34-35: Apply logic and reasoning / Draw conclusions and design a course of action

1 Responses will vary but may include: People are swimming as some are wearing bathers and goggles./They are having fun due to smiling faces./They might be in a pool as you see no beach or sand./Some are swimming in the same direction./All but two of the people in the pictures are looking directly at you./It might be pictures painted by children because of the way they are drawn.

ANSWERS

2 Responses will vary but may include:

	QUESTIONS	ANSWERS
1	Who drew the pictures and how can you tell?	Children painted the picture. I think this because of the way their name is printed on each painting/the people are painted—the arms and legs are not realistic/the water is unevenly painted.
2	What clues in the artwork tell you about what the children in the pictures were doing?	The children are swimming. Clues include: the water/the goggles and bathers/the way their arms and legs show a kicking action/the symbol on Josh and Joseph's bathers is a brand of swimwear.
3	How are the six pictures alike? List three ways they are alike.	1. They are all in water. 2. They are all happy with smiling faces. 3. They are all wearing some form of eye protection or goggles.
4	In what ways are the six pictures different from each other? List three things you notice.	1. They are not swimming in the same direction. 2. Some children are seen from the side and some from the top. 3. Some look like they are swimming and moving arms or legs, and some seem to be floating.

3 Some of the pictures can be viewed from more than one perspective.

The paintings	Looking down from above the pool	Looking up from the bottom of the pool	Looking from the side of the pool	Looking from the corner of the pool
Talia	✓	✓		
Sierra			✓	
Josh and Joseph			✓	
Adele and Breannah	✓	✓		✓

4 Responses will vary.

Page 35: Evaluate procedures and outcomes

5–6 Responses will vary.

ETHICAL UNDERSTANDING CAPABILITY

Unit 5

Pages 37-38: English – Literacy, Literature & Language

1 d

2 d

3 False – Two of the children said, 'I hate this! They will all make fun of me because I can't run.'

4 True – The teacher said, 'You all made it around the course.'

5 False – Some students are seen still crossing the finishing line while the rest of the students are with the teacher.

6 Not everyone enjoyed it because of the student comments made before the run, the look on some of their faces and the body language of the students who had finished. Other answers may be possible depending on what is observed in the cartoon.

7 Brett could have had a smug face because he expected to easily win the race.

8 Responses will vary but could include suggestions for letting children walk part of the course, starting at different times or doing a shorter course.

9–10 Responses will vary.

Pages 39-40: HASS – Inquiry and Skills

1 Responses will vary but can include: INSTRUCTIONS 1) Start at the school as everyone knows where the school is. 2) Turn left onto School Road, heading East. 3) Turn right at Main Street, heading South. 4) Turn right onto Leaf Street, heading West. 5) You will see the park on your left.

2–4 Responses may vary.

Pages 41-42: English – Literature

1 Responses will vary but may include: The cartoon is about making friends and being friendly./It is about being inclusive of others and not leaving them out./It includes being able to put yourself in someone else's shoes and think about how they are feeling./It is about how easy it is to misjudge people or make decisions about them before you get to know them. This is because the 'new kid' could play soccer, judging from the thought bubble in the last frame of the comic, especially after one of the friends said, 'He probably can't play'.

TARGETING GENERAL CAPABILITIES: CRITICAL THINKING AND ETHICAL UNDERSTANDING YEARS 3–4 © PASCAL PRESS ISBN: 978-1925726-244

2 Responses will vary but may include:

Reasons why the new kid was left out	Reasons why the new kid was included
He was new and they didn't know him.	He looked lonely.
They didn't want to bother about it.	The bell was going to ring soon, so they would only have to play with the new kid for a short time.
They thought he could not play soccer.	He had long legs and would be able to run fast.

3 Responses will vary but may include: scared, lonely, isolated, bored, unhappy, worried, excited, anxious. 4–5 Responses will vary as it depends on each person's experiences. 6 Responses will vary.

Unit 6

Pages 43-45: English – Language / Health and Physical Education – Personal, Social and Community Health 1 A rainbow is more beautiful than a sunset. – opinion/There are 26 letters in the alphabet. – fact/Not all birds can fly. – fact/Cats are easier to care for than dogs. – opinion. This one could be a fact, but factual information would need to be gathered to prove the point.

2 Responses may vary but can include:

Topics	Fact	Opinion
Visiting the doctor	You visit the doctor when you are ill. The doctor prescribes medicine when you are ill.	I like visiting the doctor because she is nice to me and is caring. I prefer being at school with my friends than being ill and visiting the doctor during the day.
Doing homework	Homework is done out of school hours and often at home. Homework is set by the teacher.	I would rather play outside than do homework. I like homework that makes me think about things.

ANSWERS

ANSWERS

3

Text	Fact or opinion?	Reasoning – Explain your reasons
We lost AGAIN Sanjay,	fact	They lost.
because Justin can't bat.	opinion	Unless the boy is a highly skilled batsman and can judge ability, it is an opinion.
He shouldn't be in the team.	opinion	Unless the boy is a highly skilled batsman and can judge ability, it is an opinion.
I think he just gets nervous during a game.	opinion	This is guesswork.
I have seen him bat really well in the playground.	opinion	What does he mean by 'really well'? Is Sanjay a good enough cricket player to judge skills?
It was awful. We might have won if I had played better.	opinion	It could be true, but it may not be the only reason why they lost. There is not enough information to make this a fact.
Out for a duck. AGAIN!	fact	The scoreboard would show this.
I thought you might like to do some cricket practice.	opinion	Starts the sentence with 'I thought'.
I have a spare bat.	fact	This is a statement and is supported by the drawing.
Really? I was thinking of quitting. But more practice might help.	opinion	It was about his thinking.
Great shot Justin!	opinion	Unless the boy is a highly skilled batsman and can judge ability, it is an opinion.

4 d

5 Responses will vary but may include: Justin felt happy. He held his bat in the air and his helmet above his head./Justin felt proud. Sanjay patted Justin on the back./Justin felt thankful for Sanjay's help. Sanjay said, 'Great shot Justin'./Justin felt excited. People at the fence held up cards to show he scored six runs./Justin felt that he had played well. Two spectators in the background had their arms up in the air.

6

The Topics	Information	Fact or Opinion?
Bananas	Bananas float in water.	fact
	To whiten teeth naturally, you can rub the inside of a banana peel on your teeth for two minutes every night.	fact
	I think bananas grow on trees.	opinion
	The only way to eat a banana split is with strawberry ice-cream.	opinion
Elephant	Elephants are afraid of bees.	fact
	Elephants don't like peanuts.	fact
	Elephants can get sunburned.	fact
	A good food for elephants is peanuts.	opinion
Hair	I prefer red hair to blonde hair.	opinion
	My hair grows faster in winter than in summer.	opinion
	Pigeon poo can be used to dye hair blonde.	fact
	Humans have the same amount of hair follicles as chimpanzees.	fact

TARGETING GENERAL CAPABILITIES: CRITICAL THINKING AND ETHICAL UNDERSTANDING YEARS 3–4 © PASCAL PRESS ISBN: 978-1925726-244

Pages 46-48: English – Literacy & Literature / Mathematics – Statistics and Probability

1 replied, cake, because, slyly, plan, brought, lying, smell

2 Responses will vary but may include: **The wolf was very hungry, so what happens next?** 'All the better to EAT you with. In the next moment, the wolf gobbled up Little Red Riding Hood, basket and all.'/**Granny is alive and baking cakes in the kitchen, so what happens next?** 'All the better to EAT Granny's delicious cakes. Let's have a glass of milk and some hot cakes, straight from the oven.'/**Little Red Riding Hood is an expert in kung fu and boxing, so what happens next?** 'All the better to EAT my last meal!' As soon as the wolf finished the sentence, Little Red Riding Hood boxed him in the face and kicked him, kung fu style, out of the house. Granny emerged from the cupboard where she was hiding and slammed the front door shut, locking out the wolf for good.'

3 According to the site https://kids.kiddle.co/Wolf#Diet, wolves are carnivores and eat meat. You can visit the site for more information.

4 The task requires information from other people, so responses will vary.

5 Answers will vary, but the expectation is that the graph resembles the example given, in its construction.

6 Responses will vary but may include: I am not bad because I was only doing what a wolf does, hunt for food. Little Red Riding Hood was in my forest and she is meat after all. I just wanted to have Grandma as a snack and finish with Little Red Riding Hood as dessert. If I am 'bad' for hunting for food, then all predators would be called bad.

Unit 7

Pages 49-50: English – Literature & Literacy / Health and Physical Education – Personal, Social and Community Health

1 i. Brett wanted to hand the money into the office. ii. Lucy wanted to keep the money and spend it. iii. Brett wanted to return the money because someone might get into trouble for losing it. iv. Lucy thought the person who lost the money should be more careful.

2 Brett

3 Responses will vary but could include: Brett was being honest, and his honesty meant that the person who lost the money could go on the excursion.

4 Responses will vary.

5 Responses may include: relieved that someone had found it/grateful that they returned the money/happy that you could go on the excursion

6 Responses will vary.

Pages 51-53: Mathematics – Number and Algebra / English – Literacy & Language

1 Responses will vary; however, the cost of all the items is to be at or under $20.

2–4 Responses will vary.

5

DAY	ADD $10 A DAY	DOUBLE PAYMENT EACH DAY
1	$10	$1
2	$20	$2
3	$30	$4
4	$40	$8
5	$50	$16
6	$60	$32
7	$70	$64
TOTAL	$ 70	$ 64

6 Responses will vary.

7

DAY	ADD $10 A DAY	DOUBLE PAYMENT EACH DAY
8	$80	$128

8 Responses will vary; however, d will earn you the most money.

9 Responses will vary depending on the answer to question 8.

10–11 Responses will vary; however, the emphasis is on honesty.

Page 54: HASS – Civics and Citizenship

1–2 Responses will vary; however, the contract will need to have parental approval.

3 Responses will vary but may include: i. help with household chores ii. don't complain about eating healthy meals iii. look after your clothes and don't lose them

ETHICAL UNDERSTANDING ASSESSMENTS

Understanding ethical concepts and issues

Pages 55-56: Recognise ethical concepts / Explore ethical concepts in context

1 Responses will vary.

TARGETING GENERAL CAPABILITIES: CRITICAL THINKING AND ETHICAL UNDERSTANDING YEARS 3-4 © PASCAL PRESS ISBN: 978-1925726-244

2

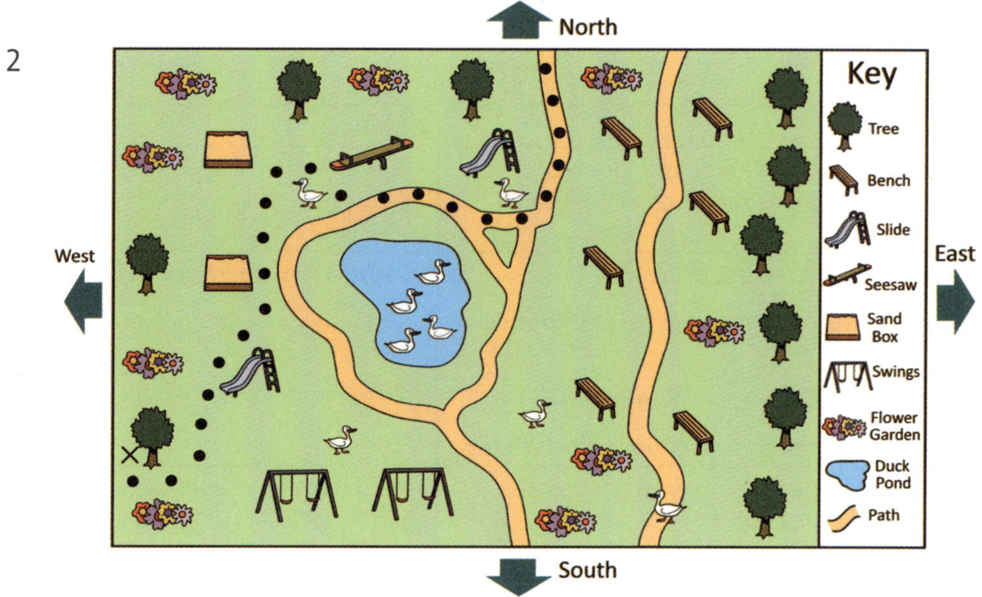

3 Responses will vary.

4 Responses will vary; however, important places must be labelled.

5 Responses will vary.

Reasoning in decision-making and actions

Pages 57-58: Reason and make ethical decisions / Consider consequences / Reflect on ethical action

1 Underlined information as follows: Two students found no lunches in their bags/ They reported their missing lunches to the principal./Principal Furrier said that he would be interviewing everyone/winter uniform is now available for sale. Contact Ms Mink (pictured here) for pricing and shop opening hours./The school canteen will be closed in Week 5/cold weather/teachers and students have been dressing warmly when they are outdoors.

ANSWERS

2

Persons Interviewed	Facts	Opinions
Inya Hood, a Year 4 student	- When Red Riding and I looked in our school bags, our lunches WERE NOT THERE!	- We think they had been STOLEN! - I bet I know who!
Mrs Lupin, a Year 3 teacher (pictured)	- It was a very cold day. - I was on my way to do playground duty. - I wore my very warm coat. - I did see my reflection in the window.	- I don't think there was a big hairy thing.
Ms Mink, the school Uniform Shop Manager	- I was just on my way to open the uniform shop. - I didn't see it. - I did overhear two of the students talking.	- They may have said something about their lunches.
Frannie Frizz, a Year 3 student	- My mum gave me money to buy my lunch at the canteen, but it was closed. - I had to go to the office to get an emergency lunch.	- I don't like them. (emergency lunches) - Inya and Red most likely thought I was the big hairy thing.

3–4 Responses will vary.

Exploring values, rights and responsibilities

Page 59: Examine values – Honesty

1 c

2 Responses may vary but can include: The villagers were angry with the boy for tricking them and so decided not to be tricked by him again./They ignored his calls thinking it was a trick.

3 Responses may vary.

Page 60: Explore rights and responsibilities / Consider points of view

1 Responses will vary but can include: **Good idea** – It's a safe place for dogs to exercise and roam freely. The dogs can socialise and mix with other dogs, and dog owners can socialise as well./All dogs are in one area which will help people who are afraid of dogs. They can avoid that area but still enjoy the park.

Not a good idea – The health of dogs is put at risk with the potential of spreading disease./Putting large and small dogs together in one area can cause rough play injuries. Aggressive dogs can cause injuries in fights./It does not provide the owner with any exercise. Walking a dog is exercise but standing and watching your dog is not.

2

How much of the park will be used for the off-leash section? YES

Will my dog behave itself in the park? NO

Will the off-leash section be fenced? YES

Would you be allowed in that section if you do not have a dog? YES

Will there be certain time restrictions as to when the off-leash part can be used? YES

What if I am scared of dogs? YES OR NO This question has points for and against being asked.

Did you make this rule because you like dogs? NO

3 Responses will vary.

Targeting General Capabilities
CRITICAL & CREATIVE THINKING AND ETHICAL UNDERSTANDING

Years 3 & 4

ISBN: 978-1925726-244

Published by Pascal Press
PO Box 250
Glebe NSW 2037
www.pascalpress.com.au
contact@pascalpress.com.au

Authors: Margaret Bishop and Susan Wilson
Publisher: Lynn Dickinson
Editor: Marie Theodore
Typesetter/Designer: Stacey Grainger
Illustrator: Paul Lennon

Printed in South Korea by Prinpia Co. Ltd.